Praise for *Confidence* by Ethan Nichtern

"In such wild times as these, this book offers us brave good medicine."

— **Jack Kornfield**, author of *A Path with Heart*

"*Confidence* is a compelling call to claim our rightful place in this life. Ethan Nichtern's clarity and compassion, paired with his humor and humility, open the heart to welcome the eight worldly winds of life in a manner that is possible for us all."

— **Sharon Salzberg**, author of *Lovingkindness* and *Real Life*

"Ethan Nichtern can turn a phrase! *Confidence* is brilliant, highly honest, very down-to-earth, and helpful to anyone who intends to live meaningfully the privilege of being human, always striving to be more so. I love Ethan's transcendent nontranscendence and strongly recommend you bring this beautiful and inspiring book into your life!"

— **Robert Thurman**, Jey Tsong Khapa Professor Emeritus of Indo-Tibetan Buddhist Studies, Department of Religion, Columbia University, and author of *Wisdom Is Bliss*

"Ethan Nichtern's *Confidence* embarks on a profound exploration of self-assurance, challenging traditional notions with a refreshing blend of personal narrative, Buddhist philosophy, and actionable advice. Ethan masterfully dissects the nuances of confidence beyond superficiality, guiding readers toward a deeper understanding rooted in mindfulness and self-compassion. His approach is both relatable and insightful, making complex concepts accessible to all. The book stands as a beacon for those navigating the intricacies of self-trust and self-worth, offering a path to genuine confidence through introspection and mindful practice. *Confidence* is a must-read for anyone seeking to embrace their vulnerabilities and cultivate a life of presence, empathy, and resilience. Ethan is a master teacher."

— **Shelly Tygielski**, activist, founder of Pandemic of Love, author of *Sit Down to Rise Up*, and coauthor of *How We Ended Racism*

"A generous, inspiring, and illuminating book that reveals the meditative path as a way not of escaping reality but of plunging more wholeheartedly into it, with all its imperfections, anxieties, flawed teachers, injustices demanding our attention, and everything else. *Confidence* is a clarifying and empowering field guide to the world in which we actually find ourselves."

— **Oliver Burkeman**, author of *Four Thousand Weeks: Time Management for Mortals*

"During this time of vast uncertainty and divisiveness, where can we find genuine confidence in ourselves, each other, and the world? With his trademark sharpness and kindness, Ethan Nichtern's new work teaches us that we can trust in the unchanging brilliance of our true nature and, in so doing, support others to do the same. Confidence, he tells us, is not about stabilizing in a superhuman place of certainty, but about holding uncertainty fearlessly."

— **Susan Piver**, author of *The Four Noble Truths of Love* and *The Buddhist Enneagram*

"This book is a masterclass in marrying vulnerability with badassery, showing us that true confidence is about leaning into our authentic selves and owning our stories, sassy quirks and all. As Ethan Nichtern shows, real confidence comes from knowing ourselves fully — shadows, light, and all. A must-read for anyone ready to live boldly and unapologetically."

— **Sah D'Simone**, bestselling author of *Spiritually, We*

"Real confidence, true confidence, comes not from a false front or a fleeting achievement; it goes way deeper than that. And Ethan Nichtern, a deft and experienced teacher, will take you there. I wish I'd had this book when I was much younger. It would've prevented me from all manner of suffering and embarrassment."

— **Dan Harris**, author of *10% Happier*

"In a world where it's easy for self-doubt to cloud our vision, Ethan Nichtern shares his profound insight and practical wisdom to illuminate the importance of cultivating confidence to navigate life's complexities. Like everything Ethan teaches and writes, *Confidence* provides clarity and overflows with compassion, making it an essential read for anyone seeking self-discovery by unearthing and unleashing their inner strength."

— **Shannon Watts**, author and founder of Moms Demand Action

"*Confidence.* We post it, we lack it, we want it, we seek it, we hoard it, we lord it, we try to buy it and, I hope, offer it to others. It's a simple word with complex origins and imprints and expectations, and we all need help with it. I'm so glad that Ethan Nichtern is offering this practical access point to confidence!"

— **Jamie Lee Curtis**

"Ethan Nichtern guides readers to a resilient inner balance while dealing with the challenges of life, and each page sings with his kind and soulful voice. With skill and grace, he brings together Buddhist wisdom, clear seeing of injustice, heart-touching examples, and practical suggestions in this timely and very useful book. It's a pleasure to read, and the benefits will ripple through your life and onward, outward to the world."

— **Rick Hanson, PhD**, author of *Buddha's Brain: The Practical Neuroscience of Happiness, Love, and Wisdom*

confidence

Also by Ethan Nichtern

The Dharma of "The Princess Bride": What the Coolest Fairy Tale of Our Time Can Teach Us about Buddhism and Relationships

The Road Home: A Contemporary Exploration of the Buddhist Path

One City: A Declaration of Interdependence

confidence

Holding Your Seat through Life's Eight Worldly Winds

Ethan Nichtern

New World Library
Novato, California

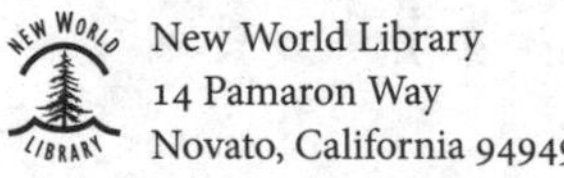

New World Library
14 Pamaron Way
Novato, California 94949

Text design by Tona Pearce Myers

Library of Congress Cataloging-in-Publication data is available.

First printing, May 2024
ISBN 978-1-60868-854-8
Ebook ISBN 978-1-60868-855-5
Printed in Canada on 100% postconsumer-waste recycled paper

New World Library is proud to be a Gold Certified Environmentally Responsible Publisher. Publisher certification awarded by Green Press Initiative.

10 9 8 7 6 5 4 3 2 1

Thinking of Claire Nichtern, this is for Izzy Atlas Nichtern.
May you hold your seat.

Contents

INTRODUCTION

Hold Your Seat

I'm not here. This isn't happening.

— Thom Yorke

My favorite song to describe exactly what mindfulness is *not* would be the Radiohead track "How to Disappear Completely." The track's refrain — "I'm not here. This isn't happening" — is an ethereal chant of alienation. The song evolves through movements of increasing disembodiment, soaring arcs that make the abandonment of life on Earth seem far more heroic and much less stressful than it would probably be. Lead singer Thom Yorke's voice grows increasingly distant and hollow as he repeats the ghostly mantra: *I'm not here. This isn't happening.* The effect is a brilliant (and seemingly self-aware) commentary on escapism. When I listen to the song's climax, a strange ambivalence pulses through me — maybe it's something we've all felt. There's a longing to be anywhere but here, any time but now, while also being haunted by the utter impossibility of that wish. I feel simultaneous tenderness for the boy in me, longing to press the reset button on the Nintendo console of life itself, and tenderness for the adult in me, who knows that life is no game.

I remember listening to this song repeatedly when the album *Kid A* dropped in the fall of 2000, right after I graduated from college. At the time, my interest in Buddhism was consuming most of my heart and brain space, but I was also scared to death of assuming my position as a grown-up on planet Earth. The song always took me away from — and then back to — the thought haunting me about my nascent adulthood: "Damn. I *am* here, and this is *exactly* what's happening. How the f-ck do I show up for any of this?"

Now, many years later, whenever I work with students of Buddhism, one generalization can apply to all the unique, eccentric individuals I meet, including myself. Most of us struggle intensely with genuine confidence. If we have confidence in one area of life (like our career), then we lack it in another (like intimate relationships). Except for the famous rappers and indicted ex-presidents among us, almost all of us struggle mightily to proclaim ourselves as confident about what we offer to this world.

Confidence is defined in the dictionary as "firm trust." Self-confidence, then, is firm trust in yourself. On the outer level, this might mean trust in your specific abilities — like public speaking or coloring precisely within the lines. But inwardly, confidence means trusting in your ability to navigate your own mind. It is exceedingly rare to meet a person who genuinely trusts their own mind, the deepest container of every single experience of our lives. Getting to know — and then trust — your own mind is the core of mindfulness practice.

Confidence isn't always what people think of when they

think of mindfulness, nor the reason why they decide to practice meditation or study Buddhism. We often start out looking to reduce stress, manage anxiety, or just generally be more grateful and present for all the little moments of daily life that we usually move too quickly to appreciate.

In talking to thousands of people over the years I've been teaching, I've found that just below an initial set of attractions to Buddhist practice lurk questions of self-confidence and self-worth. Whenever a conversation about Buddhism shifts beyond the mechanics of meditation or the intriguing realm of Buddhist philosophy, it turns to the question of living a more awakened and compassionate life. And when we start talking about life, the discussion almost always turns — implicitly or explicitly — to working with insecurity, trusting ourselves, and feeling into our own power. We end up talking about trusting the choices we make, trusting the way we speak and the things we say, dealing with the thoughts we think, and most deeply, trusting that *we will be capable of navigating the unknown*.

Self-confidence is a tender and messy topic to discuss openly. Sure, alpha males swagger and bluster their way through proclaiming confidence ("I got this, bruh!"), but for most of us, even approaching the subject makes our voices get a little quieter, as if we're asking an imaginary friend if we have permission to speak freely. This is true not only for introverts but also for those of us who consider ourselves extroverts and have been able to thrust ourselves into the visibility of public platforms and all the strange vulnerabilities that come with putting ourselves out there. I wouldn't be writing this book if confidence weren't a real — and ongoing — struggle for me. Merely addressing the topic of confidence from a spiritual perspective feels like walking a tightrope, a narrow path with uncomfortable associations on both sides.

On one side of the tightrope, discussing confidence involves admitting you feel insecure, that you don't think very highly of yourself, that sometimes you feel neither powerful nor capable. It takes tremendous openness to admit your vulnerability, to acknowledge that you might be shrouded by impostor syndrome or self-hatred. On the other side, talking about confidence brings up a fear of taking up too much space — a fear that if you project too much strength or promote yourself too strongly, you'll be perceived as arrogant, greedy, or self-absorbed. This concern is amplified in some spiritual circles by the belief that a true spiritual path should signal the death of the ego, leading you to transcend human needs, especially the need for validation or recognition. According to this view, if you aren't using your spiritual path to try to disappear completely, then you're doing it wrong. I'm writing this book because this tightrope between arrogance and self-diminishment has felt very real throughout my whole life. The Buddhist teachings have helped me turn the tightrope into a cushion — a wobbly cushion, but a seat nonetheless — from which I can navigate life with more presence and compassion.

Take Your Seat, Hold Your Seat

What I most love about Buddhism is the egalitarian nature of its core belief in human capability. We all have seeds of wisdom that allow us to become more awakened, compassionate, and adept at facing both life and death. The confidence it takes to show up to life is available to every human. We might be more or less skilled at accessing our most awakened qualities, but all of us have them. None of us is irredeemable or fundamentally broken. In the traditions I've studied, "Take your seat" is used as a shorthand instruction for arranging one's meditative posture. On the surface level, it describes the physical entry into contemplative practice. We find a long spine and an open heart, assume a confident but receptive demeanor, and balance alertness with physical relaxation. The posture was intuitively designed to balance the parasympathetic and sympathetic nervous systems and quell our "fight, flight, or freeze" response long enough to help us grow more curious and insightful about our internal experience. The posture (upright but not uptight, as my colleague and friend Maho Kawachi likes to say) is designed to help us find the physical alignment that lets us experience our mental events in a state of (relatively) nonjudgmental awareness.

But "Take your seat" has a deeper meaning that extends far beyond meditation practice. It's an empowering instruction for how to show up on this earth. "Take your seat" grants us permission to take up space with confidence — not arrogance, but a sense of worth, owning our capabilities without self-diminishment. Some of us have been trained to gobble up too many seats. And many of us have come of age with the reinforced message that even being on Earth in human form is something of which we're not worthy. "Taking your seat" is also a metaphor for claiming power that has also influenced great activists in recent generations. The United States' first Black congresswoman, Shirley Chisholm, said, "If they don't give you a seat at the table, bring a folding chair."

"Taking your seat" also has a sense of accepting — maybe reluctantly — that you can't escape being an earthling, even when it feels like you're sitting inside a dumpster fire. True presence happens the moment *after* you accept the disappointment of not being able to escape your humanity. This crucial moment of disappointment — that thudding return to earth, coming back to yourself exactly as you are — happens not just once, but repeatedly. This groundedness is exactly what Buddhist meditation compels us to embrace and, eventually, transform into *happiness*, to use an extremely controversial word. Once you accept your nontranscendence, the initial disappointment of feeling stuck with your flawed humanity turns into a deep sense of relief. You can give up trying to either disappear or become someone else. You become more able to inhabit both the joys and the frustrations of being a citizen of this planet at this time of chaos. The failure to transcend everyday experience is not the malfunctioning of practice; it's the start of the journey.

You are here. This is happening. You are of this earth. You belong here. You get a spot. This spot is yours. Claim it.

Take your seat.

There's a further metaphor related to the meditation seat. This relates to what Pema Chödrön calls "learning to stay with" your difficult experiences. At a difficult moment during mindfulness practice, you're instructed to stay nonreactively present with the felt experience. This is the hardest part of any meditation session, and it mirrors the hardest moments in life. It's the moment you want to distract yourself, flee, flail, or give up and end the session early.

The ability to stay present with a difficult moment or uncomfortable emotion is called "holding your seat." When life gets hard, it's easy to do the opposite, to lose your seat (or lose your shit, as some like to say). In meditation, the force that knocks you off your seat could be caused by an itchy nose or an overwhelming memory. In life, the disruption is often caused by something more immediate, like a text from someone you're crushing on or the threat of losing your job when you're deep in debt. Either way, to hold your seat means to remain grounded and present when your mind — or your life — knocks you around. To remain open and available when difficulty arises is to make friends with — and eventually transform — your insecurity and fragility.

Privilege and the Politics of Confidence

A *New Yorker* cartoon by Jason Adam Katzenstein depicts a white man (about my age, seemingly) out at dinner with a woman of color. He is talking enthusiastically over his wine, while she sits, silently frustrated, as if he won't let her speak. The caption underneath says, "Let me interrupt your expertise with my confidence."

Ah, mansplaining. I want to acknowledge that this entire book might be depicted in that one cartoon image. I was hesitant, as a middle-class, educated, cisgender, straight white man, to write a book about confidence and insecurity, but it felt so relevant to the Buddhist teachings, relevant to my own experience, and urgently relevant to this moment in human history. A straight white man writing a book about confidence might be an epic misread of the proverbial room. Working with my own insecurities about confidence is a dilemma that has shaped my entire personal path, and it's a topic I end up discussing with almost every student I work with as well. I don't want to dismiss anyone else's expertise. I want to maintain awareness that the words in these pages are only my subjective experience of working with self-confidence, and that my experience comes from a privileged social location, with a whole slew of blind spots that I'm working through. But here we are, so let's do this.

The older I get, the less I feel an expert at anything. But I do have relevant experience and tools for this discussion: over twenty-five years of studying the human mind intensively (especially my own) and twenty-two years working with many others on their paths. Ultimately, the pathway that leads to self-confidence is an intimate and subjective one. Confidence is personal. Nobody else can tell you how it works for you.

Just like mindfulness, confidence isn't a set state of being; it's a practice you work with daily. Mindfulness isn't about always keeping focus, nor is it about conducting yourself perfectly. On the contrary, meditation is the best disrupter of my perfectionist tendencies I've ever found. Mindfulness is about retraining ourselves to be willing to show up to the moment again and again as a practice. In the words of a sweet little chant I learned in the 1990s at a Buddhist camp for teenagers in the Shambhala community: "If you lose your mind, *come back*!" There are hundreds of meditation techniques that each have their own usefulness, but the most essential instruction of all of them might be encapsulated in that one joyful chant shouted by a group of otherwise cynical teens. If we applied the same idea to the practice of confidence, the adolescent within each of us might say, "If I lose my seat, I'm gonna show up and take it again."

Why is mindfulness such a crucial practice for working with confidence? When we practice mindfulness, we get to notice all the internalized voices that tell us we're doing it wrong. *It* generally refers to whatever aspect of being human we're focusing on. The inner critic is such a sweet little jerk. He's a kind of watchdog, a poorly trained sheriff that nobody hired. There are so many of these inner voices, and they come from an intricate web of our personal and collective histories. The Buddha called his dominant inner critic Mara. I've found it fun and helpful to name a few of my own critical inner voices. One voice tells me I'm a bad Buddhist. I call that one the Dharma Police. Another voice tells me I'm bad at being a dad. That one's named Sigmund. Another reminds me of all the ways I'm letting my friends down. But my favorite is Harold. He's an intergalactically renowned literary critic — and a dick. Harold has given every word I've ever written two out of five stars on Goodreads. (The second star is because he thinks it's sweet that I'm still trying.) There are dozens of other critics in here. And don't even get me started on Che Guevara, the inner voice who tells me I'm not doing nearly enough political volunteering to save America and, also, the world.

Because the meditation seat gives us very little to accomplish in the external world, we witness how these voices operating free of all the achievement-oriented activities we engage in when we're not practicing. When all I'm trying to do is sit on my cushion and just *be*, the voices don't go away; they get a little bit clearer. *You should just give up*, a voice says inside my skull. *Give up what?* I ask back. *I'm just sitting here, my dude, trying to be a person.*

The author Celeste Ng said that privilege is all about "who's allowed to make mistakes."[1] This statement is one of the best I've found to define privilege in relation to mindfulness

1 In this tweet, Ng was referring to Jared Kushner, the son-in-law of Donald Trump, who, during his father-in-law's misbegotten presidency, had to resubmit certain disclosure paperwork over forty times in order to serve in the White House, because he kept making simple clerical mistakes.

practice, and in relation to confidence. We all hear these voices, no matter who we are, but privilege alters the way we hear them and react to them. Privilege lends me more access to supportive resources than many people have, and those resources make it easier for me to recognize and reframe my relationship to inner critics. Also, with privilege, the voices that tell me I'm a failure are mostly internal rather than external or systemic. That's a key difference. My internal Harold isn't backed up by cultural forces that make it harder just to show up. A privileged social location changes our internalized experience of confidence and gives some of us a much greater chance to feel heard and respected — to feel a sense of belonging and willingness to take up space.

Privilege means you get more chances to try things when you're uncertain about how they'll turn out. There's no way to work toward confidence without letting yourself fuck up repeatedly. The ability to "always begin again" — as one of my teachers, Sharon Salzberg, loves to say — is what practice is all about. From a position of privilege, rather than being policed or punished — either internally or externally — for infractions or failures, mistakes will be supported and usually forgiven. Often, shortcomings are just ignored. As a result, I get yet another chance to try. That perpetual second chance is key to the growth of both mindfulness and confidence. Too often we assume that the bravery it takes to get knocked over and then take our seats again is a trait of individual perseverance and fearlessness. Getting back up is a million times easier if your environment supports the making of mistakes. We have to take privilege into account when we're talking about confidence. Otherwise we are left with a disembodied and individualistic notion of what success really means, and we end up replicating harmful patterns and systems by ignoring their effects.

Of course, many truly confident people come from marginalized social positions: think of icons like Beyoncé or Michelle Obama.[2] But we never know exactly what happens in another person's heart or mind. This apparent radiance of confidence from icons may be the result of their own spiritual or psychological development, or the result of embracing their confidence as a matter of survival. By treating the self as if it exists independently of social context, the way so much "self-help" content seems to do,[3] we end up disempowering people when we're trying to aid their growth.

I vow to be as aware as I can about the dynamics of privilege and my own blind spots while exploring the experience of confidence and fragility through the lens of mindfulness. I'll try to acknowledge the mistakes that our society has given me so much permission to make.[4]

If There's No Self, How Can There Be Self-Confidence?

Maybe you're already a little familiar with Buddhist philosophy, and you're thinking that self-confidence isn't a valid Buddhist term. You might ask, Isn't Buddhist meditation about

---

2 Michelle Obama has written extensively about her relationship to confidence. The former first lady once observed at a lecture in London that her self-doubt "never goes away." But she also said (perhaps referencing Shirley Chisholm's idea of taking a seat at the table): "I have been at probably every powerful table that you can think of, I have worked at nonprofits, I have been at foundations, I have worked in corporations, served on corporate boards, I have been at G-summits, I have sat in at the UN: They are not that smart."

3 The term *self-help* makes me cringe.

4 If this sounds like "virtue signaling" to you, then that's okay with me. Even if it strikes a performative tone, I'd rather signal virtuous intentions to care about humans than to signal indifference to them.

overcoming a sense of self, about killing our perceived self-importance, which takes us away from a hallowed inner peace? And isn't confidence really just a synonym for self-importance? There are many Buddhist teachings about *anatta*, often translated as "nonself," which sounds a lot like the negation of one's identity.

You may be surprised to learn that Buddhist philosophy does not actually question the existence of self, and it's definitely not about mutilating your ego. Classic Buddhist philosophy questions only (1) the *permanence* of identity as (2) a *singular entity* that (3) *exists independently* of a complex and interwoven environment and is (4) *more important* than other selves. Mindfulness has very little to do with ego, at least in the Freudian sense of the word. In the Freudian triptych, ego can be a healthy regulator of our lived experience. In Buddhist thought, there is a regulating aspect of consciousness that serves a similar purpose (it's called the sixth consciousness, for the Buddhist geeks out there; the first five consciousnesses relate to our five embodied sense perceptions). Self-fixation is highly problematic from a Buddhist perspective. But self-confidence is necessary for any spiritual journey.

The self is an elusive concept. The individualistic self, as an entity with complete autonomy who doesn't rely on others, simply doesn't exist. Some people still argue that Buddhism is all about individual self-liberation (most of the people making these arguments in a contemporary setting, I've noticed, tend to look like me in terms of race and gender). While it's true that mindfulness revolves around an intimate and personal exploration of our own experience, from a Buddhist perspective, that personal experience exists only in the context of *other* selves which co-create families, communities, cultures, and society. Society is a system of interdependent selves in which no particular self can be understood without reference to others. Psychodynamic theory tells us that you can't "understand yourself" without understanding your parents' selves. The same is true socially. Americans can't understand the experience of self-confidence without acknowledging the interwoven legacies of slavery, genocide, patriarchy, and capitalism. In exploring self-confidence and self-empowerment, we must take account of truths like our family histories, the cultural contexts in which we operate, race, gender, class, sexual identities, and more. What has come to be called *intersectionality* relates to the earlier Buddhist term *interdependence* or *interbeing*.

We can philosophize or psychologize about the self all day (believe me, I have). Philosophy can illuminate experience, but it can also (especially for men) be a way to avoid an embarrassing conversation: the conversation about why self-confidence is so inaccessible so much of the time. This is why self-proclaimed hardcore spiritual folks often avoid the discussion of self-confidence (dismissing it as "self-help"), preferring to engage in disembodied arguments about metaphysics, in which no personal vulnerability need be revealed. It's much easier to talk about reality as an abstraction than to discuss how awkward it feels to get out of bed in the morning and attempt yet another day of being a grown-ass person. How much philosophizing can you do in those abysmal moments when you get dumped, or your manuscript gets rejected for the umpteenth time, or when you have a chronic or terminal illness? How much philosophizing can you do when fascists try to take over your country? It's easy to throw around Sanskrit terms instead of talking about our human wounds. The conversation about confidence — or lack thereof — is an inherently awkward one, and it needs to happen in our native tongue, the language of felt experience.

Encountering Our Fragility: The Eight Worldly Winds

Have you been by a car wash or car dealership and seen those inflatable people (often called tube men) who come to life when the wind picks up and wave at all passers-by like everything in the universe is amazing, only to droop in despair when the animating breeze leaves them?[5] One moment the tube man is on top of the world, and the next he looks like he thinks he's the worst piece of shit who ever existed.

If we're going to have a real conversation about confidence, we have to admit we each have one of these little tube people inside us. We're sensitive to the tiniest signals of positive or negative feedback from the world. Someone cute smiles at you, and everything is golden; and then you get a text message containing one offhand criticism, and every drop of sunshine leaves the world. The winds are constantly blowing, and they prop us up with superficial perceptions of self-worth, only to knock us down into gloom when one contradictory experience rips through. If you've been around the block a few times, you know that no matter what you do, no matter how you try to protect yourself, the next contrary experience is always coming.

In classic Buddhism, these forces that both inflate and

5 In Japan, tube men apparently go by the name "sky dancers," which sounds like a much more Buddhist name for them.

deflate our self-regard are sometimes called the vicissitudes, but they often go by an appropriate metaphor: the eight worldly winds. They are known as winds because whenever we become attached to some plateau of stillness or ease, these experiences can knock us off balance. They can also be thought of as eight traps of hope and fear — traps we face constantly — because they're moments we either chase after or brace against. Siddhartha Gautama, the historical Buddha, categorized these eight into four couplets, in which one side represents our elation (hope) and the other our deflation (fear) — or in more extreme moments, our deepest fantasies and darkest nightmares. This framework is both ancient and timeless, because even as culture evolves and technology accelerates, not much has changed in the existential terrain of the human heart. Throughout history, other experts of the human mind have also tried to elaborate ways to describe the things we all long for, such as the psychologist Abraham Maslow's hierarchy of needs (which has some surprising parallels with the eight worldly winds that Gautama talked of 2,500 years ago).

These are the four pairs of worldly winds the Buddha described, with the first of each pair describing the experience we reach toward (hope), and the second describing the experience we desperately try to avoid (fear).

1. Pleasure/pain
2. Praise/criticism
3. Fame/insignificance
4. Success/failure

The first pairing refers to the most basic human experiences, and the last to the most general: getting the result we've been striving for, arriving at an outcome that lets us taste the fruits of labor, a moment of perceived closure and satisfaction. At the other extreme lies the fear of failure or loss, where our efforts are in vain, our project unfulfilled, and our sense of self wounded or demolished completely. These eight forces could also just be called life itself.

In classic Buddhism, the skill to recognize and face these worldly winds goes by the name *upekkha*. This term is often confusingly translated as "equanimity." *Equanimity* is almost always a head-scratcher for students who hear it. In English, it has the connotation of nondisturbance, inertia, or stillness. If you meditate for more than five seconds you come to the realization that there is no stillness in this world, either internally or externally. Relative stillness certainly exists: life in the country may be calmer than life in the city. But absolute stillness does not exist in our world. Even skyscrapers — the tallest and sturdiest objects humans have made — are built to sway in the wind.

If you're paying attention when any of these winds start to blow, you're going to feel them, and they're going to push you in a certain direction. Mindfulness is not about pretending that things don't affect you. That pretense is called avoidance, a trick that works only for zombies and AI robots. Equanimity is about realizing that *everything* affects you. We are all much more sensitive to our lived experience than we might like to believe. A better English translation for *upekkha* might be "resilience." In the context of this book, *upekkha* is the practice of holding your seat and responding mindfully to the moment, rather than reacting habitually to it.[6] The ability to reclaim this resilience when the winds start blowing is the foundation of true confidence.

---

6 This distinction — responding versus reacting — was made by the psychologist and Buddhist teacher Rick Hanson in his book *Hardwiring Happiness*.

Being nonreactive never means being passive. It means responding to your needs and wants from a grounded place, a mindset supported by awareness and intention, rather than being toppled by the fast-moving threat or promise of whatever the situation at hand might present. To hold your seat means to demonstrate confidence without bluster. This power comes from presence, from knowing that life is full of forces that can make you either howl at the wind or go hide in a corner, and understanding that these forces are never going to stop moving.

Exploration of each pair of these winds offers insights into what makes our self-regard so fragile and offers practices we can adopt when they inevitably blow through our lives. These practices haven't made my own little tube man disappear. He is still right here in my chest, an eternally hopeful little dude, nervously strapping on his backpack for his first day at the school of life, his boyish chest always inflating and deflating as the winds of hope and fear blow on through. Over time, however, the tube man has come to represent a useful compass for my journey through this life. Practice has made him more flexible, more humorous, and far more connected to others' struggles.

You can't disappear from your life in this world. As I've progressed on my path as a meditator and spiritual student, I've come to see that most of that ancient spirituality that has become so popular comes from practitioners who rejected the world, or at least rejected immersive participation in the societal structures of their day. I want to tell all the deeply accomplished spiritual masters who were also world renouncers, including the historical Buddha: I get it. I get why you left society behind. I really do. When you're overwhelmed by the pressures of the real world — when you have no idea how to be a husband or a father to your infant son — of course you'd get the urge to flee. Any one of us might relate to this longing to escape the world for greater spiritual knowledge. When we get dumped, or we realize we need couples therapy, or we have to put together a résumé, or we need to figure out what we want to express creatively that doesn't feel cringeworthy, or we try to face the political realities of a broken world — we all can have the urge to leave, to go live minimally apart from human relations, to just try to figure it all out alone. But that disappearance from society is not my path. And it's probably not yours, either. The path is the world itself.

There's no moment in which you suddenly master self-confidence. Again, confidence is a practice, not an end point. And if there is such a thing as enlightenment, then it can be defined only by a perpetual willingness to engage in the practice itself.

We are here. This is happening. Let's begin.

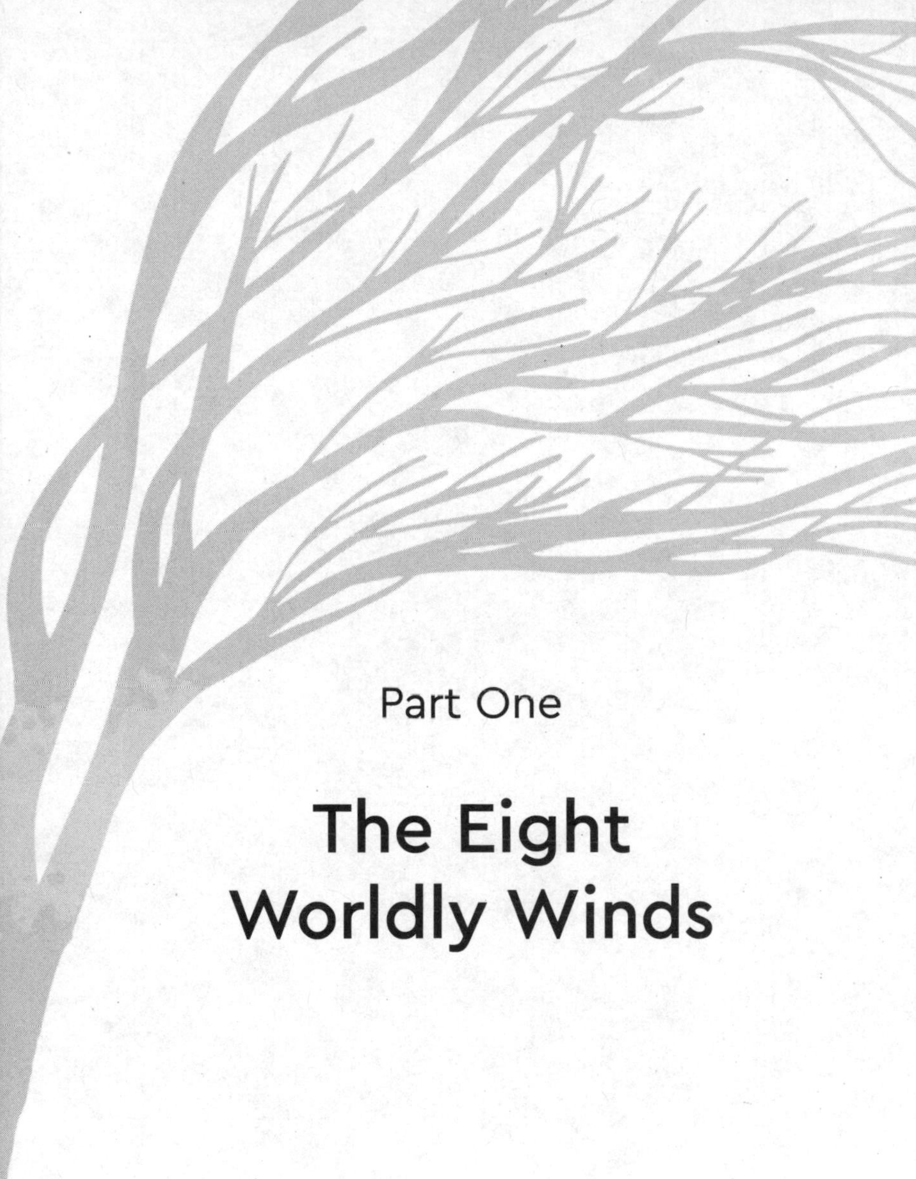

Part One

The Eight Worldly Winds

CHAPTER ONE

Running the Gauntlet of Hope and Fear

WHAT DETERMINES WHETHER THE EIGHT WINDS of the world inflate or deflate us? It comes down to two words: *hope* and *fear*. These two words summarize a tremendous amount of human experience and the way we are programmed to either chase after or fight against whatever the world serves up to us. Sometimes life provides an opportunity, and sometimes it threatens you. When we pursue an opportunity, we're running on hope. When we brace against a threat, we're experiencing fear.

In themselves, these forces are neither good nor bad. When confidence is viewed as a practice, every visit from hope or fear — and the visits are as frequent as gusts of wind — is just a chance to hold or lose your seat. When you remember to recognize and respect their place in life, these experiences become great gifts. They remind you of your vulnerability and your tender longing to be safe and fulfilled. Hope and fear are what make us all sentient beings — what make us human. The moment you were born into a human nervous system, you were guaranteed to have to work with them frequently.

For many of us, anxiety, panic, and fear — and their related stresses — are what gave us an interest in mindfulness to begin with. In recent years, the baseline anxiety of almost everyone I know has risen like the planet's sea levels (just one of many things that provokes valid anxiety about our personal and collective futures). Whether you experience it acutely or not, generalized anxiety now reigns supreme. Whether or not we've been given strategies to work with fear, we know how it can knock us off our stride, how it can paralyze and prevent us from showing up with courage and confidence to face whatever the moment presents. In each of the four pairs we'll be exploring, one side represents something we fear. In experiencing pain, we fear for our physical safety and well-being. In criticism, we fear for our reputation as a good and capable person. In insignificance, we fear being invisible, or having our contributions treated as meaningless. And in failure or loss, we fear that whatever we might build — whatever we *are* — will all come to nothing as this life comes to its inevitable end.

Our inherited cultural approach to fear is often to fortify ourselves and pretend it isn't affecting us. It's a very *Ultimate Fighting Championship* approach. *Man up, bitches!* The prevailing narrative tells us that if we were more courageous or awake, we'd be able to overcome fear, maybe even run right through it. The following reminder bears repeating ten million times, so here it is again: from the Buddhist perspective, no state of mind, no emotion, is inherently positive or negative. Every emotional state has an energy, a flavor, an intelligence, and a usefulness. A chef appreciates all their ingredients — sweet, sour, salty, bitter, or savory — to create a complete flavor profile. Being human requires a similar mixture of emotions and experiences to create a complete experience of life. We don't have to get rid of or eliminate any feeling.

If you don't know how to meet your emotions, that's when problems start. If you get stuck or fixated on an emotion (if you get too "salty," for example), or if you habitually reject or suppress an emotion, destructive patterns develop. That's when your own well-being and relationships start to suffer. Mindfulness allows you to gain more awareness of the inner terrain of your humanity and to stop ignoring emotions out of some misbegotten hope that if you ignore them long enough they'll just leave you alone. The Tibetan teacher Tsoknyi Rinpoche refers to even our most difficult, stuck, and destructive emotional patterns as "beautiful monsters." Because we are taught that fear is an ugly and dangerous monster, we never explore its energy — or its beauty — in the depth it deserves.

The Mirage of Hope

The other sides of the four pairs — pleasure, praise, recognition (or fame), and success — represent the timeless experiences every human hopes for. If you don't hope for any of these things, then (1) this isn't the book for you, and, also (2) bullshit. So what are the potential pitfalls of hope? This is a bit harder to explain than fear, because the word *hope* has generally positive psychological and spiritual associations. We associate hope with buoyancy and cheerfulness. The Buddhist teachings are defined by an abiding sense of optimism for the potential of human beings and human society. We need that positivity about ourselves and each other, now more than ever. But what happens when optimism becomes mindless or assumes a kind of "Isn't everything wonderful?" toxicity that prevents us from being honest about difficulty or disappointment? What if positivity makes us unable to face the fact that our world is literally on fire right now? What if it makes us unable to tolerate any bad news? Toxic positivity can be a form of aggression against the truth that life is hard and people suffer. It makes us unwilling to face the darker side of experience, and the darker side of the world. Hope without awareness leads to fragility when the chase goes wrong, or when the rougher facts of life — pain, miscommunication, loneliness, and loss — smack you in the face. In this sense, hope is simply fear's mirror image. If we chase our hopes just to avoid our fears, then we grow fragile, unable to tolerate the truth that life rarely gives us what we were expecting.

The year 2008 gave us an example of the complex nature of the word *hope* and our often fragile relationship to our desire. Many of us who volunteered for Barack Obama's presidential campaign experienced a sense of hope so deep that the word itself became a generation's rallying cry. The artist Shepard Fairey created a famous silk-screen poster of the dashing Illinois senator with the single word *hope* underneath in bold, all-caps type. Many friends and I rushed to volunteer and help organize for the campaign in 2007. You might remember the ubiquity of those posters, the all-caps boldness of that Gotham typeface proclaiming that marvelous little four-letter word. I have lasting memories from the two years of that campaign (American presidential campaigns are unnecessarily and profitably long) of feeling my inner little tube person rise up at the sight of those posters. We hoped to turn the page after the deeply contested election of 2000 and the events of September 11 led to so much war, misinformation, and growing inequality during the Bush/Cheney years. Many of my friends had spent the early "aughties" in protest, crying out against an inhumane war fought by the Bush administration against nonexistent weapons of mass destruction, only to have mainstream media — perhaps out of fear of seeming unpatriotic — consistently downplay the sheer size and scope of each protest. Out of all that mess, it seemed that a multiracial Black man with the middle name Hussein(!) might start laying the foundation for a new sort of democracy. Obama won the 2008 election in a landslide. Many of us danced in the streets like everybody was watching. But even in that triumph, the instability of a confused approach to hope was present.

The 2010 midterm elections happened. Many of us who were so HOPEFUL two years prior declined to show up again, either to volunteer or to vote. *You mean you have to do this every time?* We had voted our twenty-first-century knight in shining armor into office, and he'd take care of the rest, right? And then that hope was disappointed. Millions of us have since had our tube men deflated by the obstacles the American system throws up to block long-term progress, and also by the inevitable human imperfections of the chosen savior. I remember my disappointment that President Obama hadn't fought harder in 2009 for the sort of single-payer healthcare system that citizens of most wealthy countries on this planet take for granted.

The 2010 election was every bit as important to the future of America as the 2008 election had been, but the low voter turnout resulted in a Republican landslide.[1] The gerrymandered redistricting following the 2010 election paved the way for a Republican minority to reclaim power in the 2016 elections and

1 In the United States, there's no such thing as a high-turnout election where Republicans win big.

install an ultraconservative majority on the US Supreme Court, even though Donald Trump lost the presidential popular vote by three million votes. In response to Obama's historical moment, a Buddhist friend of mine — an artist with a wry sense of humor — made a silkscreen poster in the style of Shepard Fairey's iconic work, except he inserted an image of Pema Chödrön with the text beneath, which said HOPELESSNESS.

Here's the real question about our relationship to hope. The question is only two words long, and it can be applied to any and every outcome we might hope for. Even if your hopes are fulfilled — you eat the perfect meal, you land in a relationship with your dreamboat, you have perfect ease and concentration during a meditation session, your creative work wins all the accolades, your perfect leader gets elected — *then what?* Also, what if you fail? What if your dream crashes and burns in a dumpster fire, as it so often does? *Then what?* What will you do when pleasure turns to pain? *Then what?* What if the bad guys win this round? *Then what?* Either way, what comes *after* hope? How do we show up then? With any goal you might have in mind, it is worth sitting for a few moments and imagining how it will feel to achieve that goal. And after that, it's worth asking yourself this question: If this hope is fulfilled, *then what?*

When we grasp too tightly to a goal, we forget to prepare for everything that happens *after* the chase. Whether the journey succeeds or fails, there comes an inevitable letdown. Disappointment is a feature, not a bug, of human life on Earth. The fulfillment of your hopes may bring validation and temporary ease, but it doesn't resolve the human dilemma, because hope and fear will never stop visiting us. Lucky for us, human experience doesn't need to be solved or fixed.

We all need hope. I needed President Obama's style of hope after Dubya's presidency. Right now, I need the hope that my daughter will have an inclusive and sustainable world to inhabit as she takes her seat as an adult on this earth. Hope for her future gives me a daily reminder to keep showing up to this world, even when I'm heartbroken, even when a flood of items in my news feed seems to confirm the cynical notion that it's all hopeless. And, dear reader, I even need the tiny morsel of hope contained in the chocolate chip cookie I will treat myself to when I finish writing this chapter. "Chocolate-Chip Cookie Hope" gets me through the grind of long-term writing projects. Hope creates a sense of open-hearted longing, and that longing offers direction to our aspirations. We also need the validation of achieving a desired outcome, at least occasionally. Validation is crucial. If we are flattened by the constant rejection of our aspirations, how can we ever practice with confidence? Sometimes, hope needs to win out.

Hope carries the reminder and the promise of what we can achieve. But we need to remember that the winds of hope — pleasure, praise, recognition, success — are changeable. Fulfillment is always helpful, as long as our self-worth doesn't depend on the fulfilling experience sticking around forever. The false promise of hope includes a mirage of salvation, as if *this* chase is going to be the one that really does it for you, that you'll be safe forever.

Progress along any spiritual path requires us to understand that permanent salvation is a myth. No safety is permanent. If you explore modern psychospiritual methodologies — including Buddhism — this warning against overhyping temporary outcomes is crucial. I think about the mirage of hope anytime a friend dabbling in new spiritual methodologies tells me about their latest "journey" or the new practice they're trying out. Sometimes these journeys create deep insights. When the person practices whatever method they're working with wholeheartedly and consistently, you can see them moving gradually along their own path of transformation, and it's a truly hopeful experience.

But sometimes when a friend describes their latest spiritual venture — especially if the person seems to be grasping for a meaningful experience to get out of an existential rut they've been mired in — it feels like they're describing not a transformative insight but simply a dazzling moment that they're trying to hold onto and solidify. Why do we try so hard to hold onto these moments? Usually, we cling to heightened spiritual experience out of the fear that the insight associated with the experience will fade. Holding onto powerful spiritual moments creates a subtle desperation. In Buddhism, the temporary pleasant outcomes of any psychological or spiritual breakthroughs are called "peak experiences." Regarding meditation, the Tibetan tradition refers to such peak experiences as *nyam*. *Nyam* is the subtlest form of the mirage of hope, because it usually comes from a state of deep meditative concentration and absorption, which are often acquired through a lot of hard work. Peak experience — whether it's orgasm, tiramisu, or meditative bliss — feels really good. And you deserve to feel good, just like I deserve that cookie when I'm done with this chapter. The problem with focusing on peak experiences is that the good feeling can sneakily convince you that it's a transformative insight. The difference between a genuine insight and a peak experience is this: a genuine insight gives you something to revisit and work with every day of your life, while a peak experience convinces you that the work is already done. Like most other people I know, I had one or two nights in college when the MDMA released just the right amount of serotonin to convince me I was finally at one with the universe. But if that memory of open-heartedness didn't influence the way I interacted with people a week later, then I basically just spent the evening smoking hopium.

With a sense of humor, we need to question the hopeful perspective with which we pursue new spiritual approaches. Contrary to what you might see scrolling through some wellness feeds on social media, no single retreat, workshop, or experience is going to "heal" you (especially not quick-fix trademarked methods that don't have any methodological lineage backing them). Much of the time, when I hear someone promising healing, I remember the word *nyam*.[2] Awakening is a never-ending process, and healing, in my humble opinion, isn't an outcome: it is a practice that never ends.

The four positive "winds" — pleasure, praise, fame, and success — each create a mirage effect when we're not watching them closely. The four winds of fear — pain, criticism, insignificance, and failure — are the "deflating" aspects of life, the experiences we naturally avoid or try not to feel. Yet all eight experiences are parts of life that can't be avoided. Hope and fear don't need to be eliminated. They need to be recognized and

2 To be clear, teachers of Buddhism, have also inappropriately trademarked methodologies promising sudden transformations, and packaged peak experience as attainable outcomes that only *their* teaching can deliver.

befriended. As we examine each pair of winds, I invite you to contemplate how fear and hope work for you in each case. You may have a more visceral connection to one experience and a more distant connection to another. Think about what it might mean to show up fully to each — to hold your seat in the wind.

CHAPTER TWO

Pleasure and Pain

Licking Honey from a Razor Blade

We are all running from pain. Some of us take pills. Some of us couch surf while binge-watching Netflix. Some of us read romance novels. We'll do almost anything to distract ourselves from ourselves. Yet all this trying to insulate ourselves from pain seems only to have made our pain worse.

— Dr. Anna Lembke, *Dopamine Nation*

The taste of caramel versus a bite of rotten fish, the smell of jasmine flowers versus city garbage on a hot July day, the panoramic sight of a mountain summit versus a bleak layer of prefabricated concrete, a perfect harmony of choir voices versus the awful sound of an unmuffled motorcycle, playing a game on your phone versus answering work emails, the flirty touch of an attractive person versus the body aches of a newly circulating virus. Is there any experience that can make us lose our center more quickly than the "carrot" of pleasure and the stick of "pain"? In terms of the winds blowing that little tube person around, pleasure and pain are the most visceral forces of our lives, because they're experiences we all have many times each day. They are wired directly into our nervous systems, our first and foremost inheritance from the ancestry of our human lineage. Pleasure and pain usually visit us quietly, and sometimes they knock on the door *very loudly*, crowding out any other perception or thought. Take a moment to sit with your body. Are you feeling either pleasure or pain right now? Chances are, the answer is yes.

Once, on a meditation retreat where we had been working intensely with mindfulness of body practices, one of my teachers, Dr. Gaylon Ferguson, said, "Some spiritual traditions would consider the fact that we're stuck down here on Earth, inhabiting these limited bodies, as, well, sort of a drag. Some people want to transcend all that. But in our tradition, we make use of the body. We wake up through attention to the body and everything it experiences."

Pleasure and pain ground us in felt experience. The root of the word *sentient* means possessing the ability to feel. Feeling pleasure and pain return us to the very root of our biological evolution. A moment of pleasure or pain connects us to every being who has come before us. So the examination of our response to pleasure and pain is right at the root of the conversation about human confidence and what it means to take our seats as earthlings. Our senses provide the experiences that knit together the fabric of our daily lives. They're so immediate, so intimate, so inescapably real! The Buddha spoke of pleasure and pain first because they're so direct and so experiential. Before we get into the aspects of confidence that relate to social status or accomplishments, we need to discuss pleasure and pain.

One of my close friends from high school later joined the Marines and became an officer. He said that during his officer training, his drill instructor liked to say to the group: "Pain is weakness leaving the body." I was simultaneously impressed and horrified. While this quote may give us some insights into the worldview that makes the military-industrial complex possible, it's also a succinct description of how our culture teaches us to approach pain. We are taught to view pain as an insult, a failure, and — as that drill instructor said — a weakness. In her book *Dopamine Nation*, Dr. Anna Lembke takes on this mistaken cultural view and shows how our avoidance of pain detracts from our collective well-being. Out of this mistaken view an entire social and economic apparatus devoted to avoiding pain and discomfort arises. When you combine this worldview that pain makes you weak with the unending profit motives of our economic system, the brain chemicals that help us temporarily avoid pain (hey there, dopamine) become monetized and weaponized. I work with several students of Buddhism who suffer from chronic pain, and much of their work involves simply recognizing and slowly uprooting the view that their pain involves some sort of failure on their part. Pain is not weakness. Pain is humanness.

Pain and the Jedi of Mindfulness

How, if at all, does mindfulness transform our experience of pain? How might many years of practice change your brain and body's relationship to these signals from the nervous system? The best current answer to these questions may be offered by a series of experiments conducted by the team led by the neuroscientist Dr. Richard Davidson at the University of Wisconsin. The team designed experiments to track the effects of Buddhist meditation on the brain's pain receptors. The participants included people brand-new to mindfulness, people with some experience meditating, and master meditators, most notably the Buddhist teacher, monk, and author Yongey Mingyur Rinpoche.

The participants were wired up so that researchers could observe the activity in their pain receptors over a thirty-second period, broken into three ten-second intervals involving the anticipation, direct experience, and recollection of pain. At the beginning (second zero), the person was instructed that a painful burning sensation would begin soon. During only the middle ten seconds, the person was given a direct sensation of almost excruciating heat (safely designed not to cause permanent damage to the skin, even if it hurt like hell while it was happening). After the sensation ceased, the subject's pain receptors were monitored for ten more seconds.

In people with little experience of mindfulness, the entire thirty seconds were rough. The ten seconds of anticipation led to anxiety and bracing against the pain (*What's about to happen to me?*), which activated their pain receptors prematurely, and the ten seconds of reflection afterward involved reliving the experience (*That was so not cool!*). For this group, actual administration of the heat was only slightly more painful than the anticipation and reflection.

At a lecture where both were present, I heard Richie Davidson speak about Mingyur Rinpoche's experience with this experiment. Dr. Davidson described himself as initially surprised by the results. Since then, I've talked to a lot of people about this experiment, because it's so related to our understanding of how mindfulness does, and doesn't, transform our lived experience. How do you think the master meditator responded to the pain?

Most people aren't surprised to hear that Mingyur Rinpoche's pain receptors were practically inactive for the ten seconds of anticipation. He simply didn't brace against a hypothetical future experience the way the control group did, and the way most of us do. Also, perhaps unsurprisingly, his pain receptor activity was very low in the ten seconds after the sensation ceased. He didn't ruminate on the event much at all. Score two big points for meditation practice. But how did this Jedi of Mindfulness experience pain during the painful sensation itself?

For the ten seconds of actual pain, Mingyur Rinpoche's pain receptors spiked *higher* than the control group of nonmeditators. You read that right: *higher*. When it was time to feel pain, his tens of thousands of hours practice led him to feel pain even more than other participants did. "I should've known that would happen," Dr. Davidson remarked, "because his sense gates are so open." The phrase *sense gates* alludes to classic Buddhist cognitive philosophies that liken the mind to a house, and the five sense perceptions to either windows or doorways between our inner experience and the perceived world "out there."

If mindfulness practice results in a heightened experience of pain, maybe that's why so many new meditation apps and influencers say things that are slightly misleading about the benefits of meditation. "Feel pain *more*!" just isn't the slogan a modern-day Don Draper might dream up to sell subscriptions to the Calm app. But this indeed is what happens when you practice mindfulness. When the winds of pain blew through his nervous system, Mingyur Rinpoche really felt the lived experience. He was awake, and he was alive. He took his seat and held it. And holding his seat meant letting the winds of pain blow through him fully, instead of numbing out or running away, instead of treating the sensation as some punitive weakness or pretending there was no wind at all.

Coke-aine and Smartphones

Here's a memory that will always be with me on my path. I was in my early twenties, sharing a ride home from my first month-long meditation retreat, after living at a meditation center for seven months. I had done shorter retreats before, but this was a *month*. I was leaving retreat, *and* I was leaving the practice center after living and working there for so long. What was it like to meditate for a month? It was painful, it was pleasant, it was insightful, it was boring, I had a crush, I got over that crush, I wrote entire volumes of poetry scrawled on summer clouds floating in the northern New England air. I was living my best life, inhabiting a platformed tent on a frequently muddy hill, reading myself to sleep by the light of a kerosene lantern. The retreat ended in the first week of September 2001, and now I was headed home to New York City.

My ride stopped at a gas station in Vermont. I decided to buy a Coke to celebrate my return to the "real world." When I was a kid, a classmate had convinced me that Coke and cocaine came from the same plant, and sometimes cocaine ended up in Coke bottles by mistake. If you drank Coke, you had to be careful if you didn't want to get arrested, and also if you didn't want to die. Maybe this kid was in your class, too.

After a month of drinking water and coffee and the occasional yummy (but low-sugar) baked goods that the retreat center's kitchen prepared for us, this playground myth seemed to come alive in my body. A few sips into the half-liter bottle of Coke, dopamine cascaded through my brain. I felt higher than I'd ever been on those Ecstasy pills I took in college. The Coke was too overwhelming even to register as a pleasant experience. It was *aggressive*. I remember thinking to myself, as we made our way down I-91, as I fell in love again with the lushness of a summer's end in New England: *Everything in this world is four times brighter, louder, faster, sweeter than it needs to be because they're only expecting us to pay one-quarter the attention.*

It bears repeating that neither pleasure nor pain is inherently bad or good. We all need pleasure to appreciate our humanity. And there is no "grin and bear it" teaching about pain in Buddhism. If pain becomes a medical concern — especially if it becomes chronic — we need to take the steps at our disposal to relieve the pain and return the body to a state of workability. I'm certainly not the one to lecture anyone on pleasure seeking, as long as you're not harming yourself or others. But how do our brains and minds relate to pleasure and pain? How does addiction begin?

The human nervous system was slowly molded by evolution to become efficient at spotting threats to our survival in highly dangerous environments. It wasn't designed to be chill. As Rick Hanson notes in his foundational book *Buddha's Brain*, the signals of pleasure and pain are the result of the nervous system trying to get us to quickly either engage in experiences that may aid survival or avoid situations that might be life threatening. Therefore our brains are wired to exaggerate the significance of momentary pleasure and pain. And that is the basis of the hope and fear contained in pleasure and pain.

Pleasure is falsely experienced as a sense of lasting safety. And it really does feel that way when I crave a sweet thing: if I can just have this one cookie, I might reach the promised land. Conversely, each sensation of pain is interpreted by the brain as a potential threat to survival. In a world where direct and immediate threats to survival occur less frequently (for most of us who are privileged, they are rare), a world with rapidly accelerating technology and the profit motive of capitalism on steroids, these nervous system functions are fertile ground for addictions of all kinds.

If our brains aren't outright lying to us about the meaning of pleasure and pain, they are at least exaggerating what's at stake. Anyone who has felt an itch during a meditation session knows how this works. An itch is unpleasant by evolutionary design. I remember — as a reasonable grown-up — having this thought during meditation: *If I don't scratch this itch, I'm definitely gonna die.* But I chose not to listen to the message, because I had trained enough to cultivate a disbelief in the perceived urgency of passing reactions. I knew my meditation practice was the place to practice holding my seat when these momentary signals of minor pleasure and pain blew through me. And behold! A few minutes later, the itch had completely abated. It turned out my brain was misleading me, not about the fact that my body was having an unpleasant experience (it most definitely was), but about how much existential meaning could be attached to that particular sensation. We aren't misperceiving pleasure and pain. They are real human experiences. What we often do is misperceive their significance.

For a person with trauma, what gets stored in the nervous system isn't just evolutionary history, but personal and intergenerational histories of threat response as well. In his groundbreaking book on racialized trauma, *My Grandmother's Hands*, the counselor Resmaa Menakem looks at how trauma lives in the body, especially the bodies of Black and white Americans affected by hundreds of years of racial brutality and systemic white supremacy. Regarding the traumatized body's tendency to provoke an overreaction to a perceived threat, Menakem writes: "Such overreactions are the body's attempt to complete a protective action that got thwarted or overridden during a traumatic situation. . . . It then develops strategies around this 'stuckness,' including extreme reactions, compulsions, strange likes and dislikes, seemingly irrational fears, and unusual avoidance strategies. When these strategies are repeated and passed on over generations, they can become the standard responses in families, communities, and cultures."[1]

Intergenerational and racial trauma don't affect us all in nearly the same way, but we each carry the coding of both our

---

1 If you are a person with trauma working with meditation, a gentle approach is key. A few resources which might be helpful are Menakem's *My Grandmother's Hands*, David Treleaven's *Trauma-Sensitive Mindfulness*, and of course *The Body Keeps the Score by* Bessel van der Kolk. The most important thing is to connect with community and guides with whom you can work in a feeling of relative safety. Meditation techniques are often misinterpreted as one size fits all. This is not helpful; nor do I believe it was ever how Buddhist meditation was intended to be taught. Each student has their own path, and it's crucial to explore different contemplative techniques and approaches to find what works best for you.

inherited and our evolutionary responses to pleasure and pain. The past has gifted us with habitual reactions to pleasure and pain that we have no choice but to experience directly. Now, when I meditate, I'm able to develop compassion for the source of this crazy thought about my itchy nose. Somewhere in my evolutionary ancestry — I imagine — a being related to me had an itch that would not go away, an itch that persisted and could not be dismissed. Perhaps this itch came from an infection, or a snake bite, or whatever prehistoric mosquitoes did when they came upon the fresh meat of the early humans from which I'm descended. Perhaps this itch led to a close call with mortality, or even a premature death in my ancestor's group, and that tragic information was stored and passed down in the bodies of my predecessors, all the way down to me. When I feel my nose itching, I can acknowledge every ancestor who came and survived — and didn't survive — before me. Those who survived did so, in part, because they were hypervigilant and overly neurotic about the existential meaning of an itchy nose. I can also have a tender sense of humor about the absurd thought that this itch might kill me. After all, it seems credible, from the perspective of evolutionary biology, that the ancestors who survived to pass their systems along to me were generally the more nervous ones. They were the most bracing, the most defensive — the ones who scratched all the itches and overprotected their interests, even if it meant they could never find any rest or experience true vulnerability. So that I could be here, my ancestors grew fearful and defensive toward the meaning of momentary discomfort. Self-compassion begins with the full acknowledgment of your inheritance.

Meditation can be a great way to work with the winds of pleasure and pain precisely because we practice in a setting and posture where it's generally safe. When our bodies are secure and grounded and we're *still* getting strong physical signals of threat, unease, and agitation, we can see the brain's inherited trickery at play. In meditation, the mind rattles off threats and escapist fantasies in a seemingly endless supply. If there's no obvious threat, what grabs our attention are the minor itches and aches and ouches, along with the possibility of bigger ouches that might come along. Most meditation sessions are a seesaw back and forth between itches and ouches and fantasies, alongside an entire social media feed of existential observations to fill the vast space of awareness, smattered with forgotten items on the to-do list, speckled with all the unfinished business that wasn't pressing before we sat down but now somehow assumes life-or-death importance. When we slow down, we can see that many of the observations we attach to raw experiences don't mean what we thought they did.

The Dopamine Dystopia: Honey from a Razor Blade

A classic Buddhist teacher named Shantideva referred to the mindless pursuit of pleasure as "licking honey from a razor blade." I've always appreciated the seventh-century punk-rock poetry of this phrase. It could just as easily be a Nirvana lyric. The razor blade is the truth of impermanence, always lying at the bleeding edge of each pleasant experience we chase. Pleasure is historically designed to convey an experience of potential well-being and freedom from danger (Rick Hanson talks about pleasure as a signal to "approach" an experience or object that may aid survival), but our brains can trick us into thinking the pleasure will somehow make our well-being permanent.

Physical safety can never be guaranteed. Like everything else, moments of dopamine release that promise lasting ease are going to fall apart into disappointment. And when we aren't deeply aligned with that impermanence, our mindlessness is going to cut us deeply, where it really hurts. When you forget impermanence, pleasure becomes puppetry, and you're never the one holding the strings.

Let's consider what's happened to our twenty-first century world. Let's have a little compassion for the landscape we've inherited and the society we've created. Forgive me if you've already reasoned your way through the potent dystopia we've built. Almost twenty-five years after my Coke-aine moment following my meditation retreat, we're in a brave new world of dopamine delivery systems. The technology of the 2020s is far more sophisticated than almost all the sci-fi my generation thought would become reality as we aged. Instead of crudely envisioned flying Deloreans, we got the pervasive advances of the internet and the invasive connectivity of social media, algorithms, and AI.

There's good news in all these advances: they help us stay in touch with the world in ways we never used to dream were possible. We can follow the lives of people we haven't seen since high school. We can Google the net worth, shoe size, and dating status of our favorite actor while we stream every episode of the new show they're starring in. We can discover artisanal interests and participate in emergent communities based on our gorgeously nerdy eccentricities. We can follow social revolutions happening on the other side of the planet and keep track of global events in ways we never could when all we knew of the world was what the morning newspaper told us about yesterday's news cycle. We can learn to grow our own kombucha and find out whether narwhals are real or imaginary.[2] We can build a platform for our work and grow our reputations. We can share and promote all our good efforts. And through the connections we make online, we can build new political movements and replace outdated models of democracy. And for better and worse, we can slide into each other's DMs and ask a person out on a date without ever having met them in person.

But what else has happened to us? Just as the brutal enslavement that supported the sugar trade in the Caribbean a few hundred years ago was driven by a marked increase in the European consumption of sugar, our consumption of technology has led to intense and widespread suffering. Much of today's consumer technology is produced under a system of profit and forced labor, as well as unsustainable resource usage. We've become psychologically entwined with devices that lose their electric charge all too quickly, yet run on the fuel of human anxiety and discomfort. Thanks to those devices, we can microdose dopamine at all hours of the day and doomscroll on cortisol all night, while anxiety about the world and our place within it ransack our bodies and steal our sleep.

Some of the brightest psychological and creative minds of my generation — many of them my friends — have gone to work for tech giants because they couldn't forge a livelihood in an expensive American city as the artists, social workers, or academics they once dreamed of being back in school. In an

2 The narwhal's horn is actually a tooth growing outside its skull! My daughter taught me that. You're welcome.

alternate life, I could very easily have been one of them.[3] Most of us rely on social media platforms to spread the message of whatever work or news we want to share. And when we're not promoting ourselves, we're watching, endlessly observing, ceaselessly voyeuristic. Our discomfort with space has been encoded, rendered mathematical and algorithmic, weaponized and fed back to us, ad by eerily personalized ad, click by nervous click, scroll by anxious scroll. Many of us are convinced our devices are listening to our offline conversations, because when we go online, we are offered exactly the item we were just casually discussing with the humans with whom we still manage to interact in flesh and blood.

Out of the profitable march of technological platforms, a tiny group of men with truly unfathomable resources and decidedly poor social-emotional skills have been put in charge of the way most people on the planet consume data and connect with each other. In a more compassionate world, management of these socially connective arenas would draw on — and nurture — precisely the heart-based skills and moral compass these men tend to lack. Instead, anxiety and depression have skyrocketed — especially among adolescents and most especially adolescent girls. The limbic activation that these platforms require for maximum views and clicks has also become fertile ground for spreading fascist and white supremacist dogma. Online platforms have fostered bogus populist ("astroturf") movements backed by oligarchs that have toppled multiple democracies and threatened to topple the United States, which — at this writing — hangs on by its fingernails. At the

3 The popular HBO comedy *Silicon Valley* featured a billionaire tech CEO who employed a spiritual guru. Maybe, in an alternative timeline, I'm that guy.

root of this system is the false promise of a mistake our nervous systems have been making for millennia. We mistake a momentary hit of pleasure for some lasting salvation, some final escape from our personal and collective restlessness.

I'm far too interconnected with the people who work for these platforms to separate myself from them without being a total hypocrite. I use social media — less than I once did, but I use it. I try to use it with intention (though *intention* is a word that's never easy to define and always messy to live by), but I'm there, alongside all the other influencers and entities vying for all the suffering eyeballs attached to all the humans blown about by the winds of hope and fear. And just like anyone else, I'm regularly swayed by the promise that this next random scroll will once and for all resolve my discomfort with being an aging human being stuck in a slightly uncomfortable body.

We are all in this spiritual dilemma together, and any solution to our personal and collective problems needs to acknowledge that basic truth. Our world is fundamentally the same realm of which ancient masters of the mind spoke when they turned their attention to humanity's fragile relationship with pleasure and pain. If in seventh-century India the mindless quest for pleasure was like licking honey from a razor blade, then today the chase for dopamine is not a solitary cut by one razor blade but a slow-moving torture by a million micro-incisions.

It's interesting to imagine an experiment analogous to the neuroscientists' thirty-second exploration of pain. We could hypothesize the response of a mindful person to an interval of strong pleasure or dopamine release. How would you respond to ten seconds of intense pleasure if you knew for sure that it would end as quickly as it started? How would I respond to being given a single bite of my favorite dessert if what I wanted was an entire bowl? When I reflect on my own experience before and after a pleasant moment, it's often tinged with an unsettled feeling similar to the period before and after pain. If someone handed you your smartphone for ten seconds and then took it away, how would you work with those feelings?

In the period before pleasure hits, we're expectant, often hoping no one notices our minds plotting secretively toward the object of desire. After it's gone, we may have genuinely appreciated the moment; but we might get stuck in lament, wondering why the dopamine hit had to be so damn fleeting, wondering how to get more. And yes, while I'm eating that cookie, I do find the taste brilliant and soothing, but even in moments of orgasmic bliss, the mind sometimes distracts itself and meanders elsewhere, unable to hold its seat with the full intensity of the direct experience.

Mindfulness brings a clearer understanding of pleasure. It's possible to notice the longing for future pleasure without thirsting like an unemployed vampire for it. It's possible to let go a little more easily after the pleasure is gone. And what about during the pleasant interval? That bite, that payoff, that moment that is supposed to do it for us, whatever *it* may be? How might a more awakened person handle that? Extrapolating from my own experience on the path and the Buddhist teachings themselves, I imagine that the pleasure center of the Jedi of Mindfulness has been honed over thousands of hours to experience the moment far more fully than that of someone who can't hold their seat. Just as with pain, it's possible she can taste the honey more intimately, more fully, and more appreciatively, and when dopamine is released in her brain, her awareness wavers far less than that of a person constantly blown around by the quest for those sweet little neurotransmitters.

In the Tantric Buddhist tradition, the most evolved relationship to the twin experiences of pleasure and pain is referred to as an experience of "one taste."[4] While the ability to experience this consistently is often considered a very advanced meditative state, it's an experience we can touch at any time. "One taste" occurs when we have an appreciation for both pleasure and pain such that the mind is no longer favoring one over the other. In the space of "one taste," whatever the current feeling may be — whether it's pleasant, unpleasant, or neutral — we experience deep curiosity and appreciation. Above all, the experiences of pleasure and pain remind us of the beauty of being alive.

In *Dopamine Nation*, Dr. Lembke describes the experience of pleasure and pain as colocated, meaning they occur in overlapping segments of the brain. She speaks at length about the healthiness of balancing the two in our experience. She uses the analogy of a mindless approach to pain and pleasure being like an erratic seesaw, a seesaw that is most stable when the pleasure and pain sides are in balance. She says: "It wants to remain level, that is, in equilibrium. It does not want to be tipped very long to one side or another. Hence, every time the balance tips toward pleasure, powerful self-regulating measures kick into action to bring it level again." Mindless repetition of a pleasurable activity (say, clicking or scrolling) diminishes the

---

4 Tantric Buddhism is also called Vajrayana Buddhism, referring to the practice and philosophical traditions that historically flourished in Tibet and the Himalayan region.

pleasure it brings, while the pain of craving (which Lembke calls the "gremlins" on the other side of the seesaw) gets worse and worse.

Shantideva's razor blade analogy doesn't mean we shouldn't lick the proverbial honey from time to time. It just means we should know the potential danger in what honey does for us. We understand pleasure as an experience fundamentally boundaried by an inability to maintain it. We cannot tip the seesaw to one side for too long. Pleasure is unstable because it is defined as an experience relative to pain. When we remember this instability, the honey offers the exquisite appreciation of the fact that we're earthlings. Through the experience of "one taste," the strange process by which honey comes into being becomes much easier to appreciate. Rather than just focusing on the hit of sugar, we appreciate this gorgeous substance that is not quite, but almost, bee vomit. The fact that humans can gain such exquisite joy from a bee's secretions is worthy of at least a few moments of wonderment.

Holding Your Seat Means Being Uncomfortable

"I'm borrrrrrred!" my daughter (who was only eighteen months old when she intuited how to tap the "Skip ad" button as we watched lullaby videos on YouTube) will exclaim sometimes. It's during a moment of anchorless space in between events when her chosen activity has lost its shimmer, and no other worthy venture has arisen to seize her attention. Her boredom isn't bad news. Although my daughter has a seemingly endless curiosity about the world, she has not yet developed much curiosity about her own boredom. (I certainly don't expect her to yet; I didn't until much later on.) "I'm bored" comes in those moments where she feels the restless discomfort of being, an existential dilemma that, after seven years and counting in her body, she is only beginning to relate with. Those are moments that even us big kids are poorly equipped to handle.

Perhaps the most interesting marker of our existential insecurity can be seen in those moments where we aren't experiencing either pleasure or pain. Pleasure gives us something to grasp onto, and pain gives us something to fight or brace against. Both "winds" make us feel alive and real. Both give us the illusion of knowing where we stand. Pleasure and pain are programmed evolutionary responses, even if those responses aren't always helpful to our well-being. But in a neutral space, we don't know where we stand, and we don't know what to do. We don't even know who — or if — we are.

In Buddhism, this not-knowing is correlated with the experience of space — not *Star Trek* space, but the space in between defined and familiar experiences of selfhood. That experience of space becomes uncomfortable quickly, precisely because it's so undefined. Yet it is something we all need to befriend. I discuss it more in chapter 8, on awareness.

I often joke that in an enlightened world, car horns wouldn't make loud, disruptive noises. If you laid on the horn for too long when you were stuck in traffic, a child's voice would speak gently from your car to everyone else on the road, saying "Sorry, everybody, I'm uncomfortable right now." When I hear my daughter telling me she's bored, I hear my own inner child, not knowing what to do or who to be to prove that he's real. Just imagine where our planet would be if human beings — especially humans with power and privilege — could more often say, "I'm uncomfortable, and I don't know what to do about it." Just imagine if we could extend this same vulnerability and honesty not just to our physical restlessness but to the pain we feel in discussing difficult topics like privilege, fear of intimacy, fear of trying something new, and most importantly, fear of death.

The Practice of Feeling What You Feel

The practice of mindfulness starts with the simplest building blocks of honest attention, which then lead to simple insights that we find in the smallest moments of life. Exploring how we respond to pleasure, pain, and uncertainty opens the door to understanding how we can hold our seats in the face of hope and fear, especially when encountering the duality of praise and criticism.

There's a classic mindfulness meditation on feelings that's incredibly useful because it's also incredibly simple. It helps us gain insight into pain, pleasure, and the uncomfortable space in between. It is the second way that the historical Buddha taught mindfulness meditation, after he taught attention to the breath and the experience of the body. The practice is straightforward. In this exercise, you sit more openly, observing your senses and thoughts as they arise, and note your moment-by-moment experience with just three labels: pleasant, unpleasant, and neutral. You don't elaborate or analyze more than that. You don't try to get to the root causes of your pleasure and pain, your socialization, or your trauma. You simply sit and observe experience arising, being, and changing into something new. You place those three labels on your momentary experience and see how it goes. You get to watch a live-action picture of what your mind and body do in response to these momentary signals of pleasure and pain.

The name of this technique, *vedana*, is perhaps best translated as "mindfulness of feeling tone." It reveals the most basic layer of our sensitivity to the world and the roots of our human inheritance. If the human nervous system were a computer code, then pleasant, unpleasant, and neutral reactions would be like the zeros and ones and nulls of that code. There are only three options, although they may alternate rapidly. This sip of coffee is either pleasant (yes), unpleasant, or neutral. This thought of a tabby cat is either pleasant (if you love to snuggle with cats), unpleasant (if you're allergic or just had to clean a litter box), or neutral (if you consider cats the disaffected hipsters of the animal world). It's that straightforward. You note pleasant, unpleasant, and neutral responses and then do the same for the next moment.

When I practice this "feeling tone" meditation, either formally or while moving through my day, I'm humbled by how simple and universal it is to be human, and how oriented we all are to these basic signals of threat and safety. Pain hurts, neutrality is boring, and pleasure makes me lose my chill. You can feel each experience happen without being a puppet to it. Without close observation and acceptance, such experiences make us lose our seat constantly, because they each deliver a force. With mindfulness and acceptance, we give ourselves the chance to respond more effectively to what our nervous system throws at us. I honestly don't know how I would do in Dr. Davidson's pain experiment. Progress in these practices is decidedly nonlinear. My mindfulness practice certainly came in handy during a recent hour-long fMRI. Afterward, the technician told me I lay more still than almost anyone he'd seen during the procedure. (I got caught up in this moment of praise, but that's for the next chapter.) It was nice to hear this validation, because internally I almost completely lost my shit at the beginning. I was gripped by an intense wave of claustrophobia as my head and body slid into the machine, which my nervous system understandably mistook for a coffin. I credit my ability to stay in the MRI to exactly these mindfulness practices. I tried to pay close attention to the strange new world inside that machine with all its fascinating sounds, as if my brain was in the midst of a gut renovation overseen by a team of invisible dwarves. I was able to take an interest in what was happening to me. "I'm more present than I used to be" is the only thing I can say when people ask about my own progress with mindfulness.

I suggest an experiment: do this meditation of noting pleasant, unpleasant, or neutral for a few minutes with your smartphone positioned right in front of you. Just place it on the desk or floor. Then, without interacting with the device, track your bodily response as you visually examine the object. What associations does the device bring up in you? Notice those feelings in the body. Next, mindfully pick the device up and interact with one of the apps you use daily (and perhaps, shall we say, not so mindfully). Stay as present as you can while you navigate the app. How do clicking and scrolling feel in your body? Pleasant? Unpleasant? Neutral? If it's pleasant, how long does that feeling last after a single click or scroll? Does the pleasant sensation linger? Or does it fade immediately, requiring another click, scroll, or app for you to feel soothed again? If the sensation is unpleasant, ask yourself the same questions. How long does it linger?

When Dr. Judson Brewer, author of *The Craving Mind* and

Unwinding Anxiety, developed a successful mindfulness intervention for smokers, he had them focus on slowing down and examining the actual experience of each embodied movement: each reach for the cigarette, each motion toward the lips, each puff, and the *felt experience* after each puff. We could do the same practice with our devices. It turns out that most people experience the act of puffing itself as *unpleasant*, for the simple reason that cigarettes taste like shit. They soothe an itch in the nervous system, but the delivery of the soothe isn't exactly pleasant. Similarly, most of the time, when I casually grab my phone, it's an anxious experience for me, and the soothe that I get from connecting with the "world" at my fingertips is more than offset by all the anxieties and obligations that this atmosphere of overconnection carries with it. In your own mindfulness practice, you may find something different for yourself about how you relate to your device, and that's great. But when I use my phone, I have to remember that the device is highly useful as a tool for connection, but using it is also an unpleasant bodily experience, one defined by anxiety and grasping. I try to use my devices with the clear purpose of connecting with others, and I have to use them with a lot of mindfulness. The addictive structure of the device is a feature, not a bug, and it works against my well-being. As much as possible, I try to avoid using my phone to scratch the various itches that it was designed to provoke rather than to soothe.

Contentment

I once had an experience almost too simple to describe — but transmissions of true wisdom often carry a sense of ineffability. We therefore end up describing simple moments as poetically as we can, but most of these moments end up in the category of "you kind of had to be there." I had the opportunity to stand just a few footsteps from the late Zen master Thich Nhat Hanh, then eighty-seven years old, as he gave a calligraphy demonstration in New York. I had heard Thay speak several times before, but I'd never been this close to him. Watching his body and hands execute each brush stroke was magical enough, but the most memorable part of the experience had nothing to do with the calligraphy. It was how Thay related to his thermos and cup of tea. Suffice it to say I've never seen a person enjoy a cup of tea quite like that. He was effortless and present with the warmth and flavor. His hands treated the cup like the vessel itself was alive and wanted to be loved, just like everyone else.

There is no moralizing here, and I'm not a monk: I believe that some of us could be just as present with a glass of wine or whiskey, and definitely with a chocolate chip cookie. (And I absolutely believe it's possible — albeit much harder because you're working against the intentions of app designers — to be present with your smartphone, if you remember your intention to connect and feel your feelings as they arise.) Thay wasn't mistaking the experience of touch and taste as things that needed to be augmented or intensified. There were no additives. He was experiencing the union of love for his humanity and love for the objects that help a human survive and thrive. I remember his sense of fluid satisfaction with each sip. He was demonstrating that experience of "one taste." *He gets to feel like this every damn day*, I thought.

I have complete confidence that Thay died with that same curiosity and appreciation, too.

CHAPTER THREE

Praise and Blame

Everyone's a Critic

You look beautiful! | Oh, you're wearing *that*?

You're such a considerate roommate. | You never wash a single damn dish.

You really killed it. | You totally blew it.

I admire your bravery in speaking your mind. | Honestly, you need to learn when to shut up and listen sometimes.

Darling, your presence lights up the room. | Honey, you take up too much space.

Your confidence inspires me. | You're such an arrogant prick.

You really know how to hold space for others. | You seem distant and withdrawn.

You're so incredibly authentic. | You're so fake I can't stand it.

I respect your ability to set clear boundaries. | You're never there when I need you.

This is a really polished effort. | Your work…needs work.

We stan a legend! | We can't stand you.

You slay. | You're trash.

Praise and blame. Compliment and criticism. This is the second coupling of the winds of hope and fear that can knock us off our seats. The perception that we're being either praised or criticized can reveal vulnerability — and fragility — more directly than any other human experience. Unlike pleasure and pain, which can course through the body whenever our senses are open and operating, praise and blame happen in the context of social interactions. Because we're deeply relational beings, the feedback we get from — and give to — other people is intimately tied to our feeling of self-worth. In an interconnected world, we are mostly "selves" in the context of our social relationships. Of course, those criticisms are often internalized, voiced as private thoughts and narratives (the "inner critic"), but those inner critics are still a product of the feedback we receive in our social experience starting from a very early age.

There's no way to exist in the world without receiving feedback from others. Parents, children, partners, students, teachers, bosses, employees, clients, neighbors, friends, editors, landlords, and all the random people you interact with can and will each tell you what they think of what you've done, what you should be doing, and who you are. Feedback can be incredibly valuable, but it can also be debilitating if you don't have a good understanding of how to practice giving and receiving it.

One time I got feedback from a friend and teaching

colleague who was Black and queer. At the time, the organization we were both part of, Shambhala International, was in the process of collapsing because of credible sexual misconduct allegations against the head of the worldwide community, Sakyong Mipham. There were also a lot of other problems with the organizational hierarchy that were becoming increasing obvious. Although I was quite removed from the core of the structure and the actions of its central figure, I was a local leader and therefore responsible for enabling a good bit of the organizational and communal issues myself. A lot of us were soul searching, trying to figure out our role within a complex spiritual system and to discern where we'd each go from here. Publicly and privately, I had invited feedback from others about the way I had showed up in the organization and community. My colleague and I had done good work together on the local level, and I trusted their take, which was usually loving and playful, yet sharp and bullshit-free.

In an email, my colleague and friend spoke appreciatively of me but also offered this: "[I've heard from multiple people that] because you have yourself in the 'good white guy' category, you sometimes think you know more than you actually do about the lived experience of those with different embodiments." For a few moments, the email stung, and I had to think deeply about why. It didn't bother me particularly to be lumped together in a somewhat critical manner with other men, especially white men. As much as this era of scrutinizing privilege has made me face my discomfort and acknowledge my blind spots, looking at deep issues systemically has also brought a sense of relief. Patriarchy and white supremacy are systemic problems, not personal shortcomings. Addressing them is not a matter of assuming the defensive posture required to maintain your status as a "good" individual — although accountability for personal behavior is key. It's about seeing how entire systems of harm, vast forces to which we've grown blind, live within each of us. These systems give us huge blind spots in order to maintain their (dys)functionality. To take the calling out of systemic oppression as some sort of personal attack against "me" is a mistake we white men make far too frequently, and it's an entirely unnecessary reaction, although it's an understandable one when any human feels blamed for causing suffering. But we can move beyond personal blame or credit for the world. We can acknowledge how the system lives within each of us without trying to prove that we are "good" individuals within the system. Who would want to be a "good" person within a bad system, anyway? What would that twisted credential even offer to you?

Hoo boy, do I know the general blind spots associated with my particular group. Sure, we're not all Harvey Weinstein, but I've seen our behaviors and enacted many of them myself. I've heard oh so many stories. In 2016 two-thirds of American white male voters chose as their president a bankrupt, criminal reality-TV star, someone credibly accused of twenty-six sexual assaults, because he knew how to tug at all our insecurities, and he knew how to reframe the avoidance of those insecurities as a patriotic quest for some long-lost "greatness" and "freedom." Other white men — many of whom wouldn't admit that they're part of the same movement of white male individualism — have taken up this individualistic cry as well. Those of us in the remaining third of white men who try to separate ourselves from that movement can at least acknowledge that we engage in *some* of the same behaviors because they're what we've been socialized to do. For me, being typecast as a member of my group is a minor annoyance, a hurtful moment I can safely investigate with mindful reflection. For others, being typecast — such as a Black man pulled over by police for driving with a broken tail light — is a potential threat to survival.

From a Buddhist perspective, every person is basically good, even if they don't have the tools to recognize that goodness in this lifetime. (Yes, even Donald Trump.) We all have the seeds of awakening within us. And that fundamental truth is not altered or threatened when someone who cares about you points out with love that you gain problematic comfort and blind spots within an oppressive system. Sure, perhaps people who don't care about you and aren't in a place to speak insightfully have given you some rough feedback about your privilege that was clumsily delivered or overly generalized, and it stung. But these minor ouches are an exceptionally small price to pay for the difficult long-term conversations it takes to build a more compassionate world, aren't they?

I knew all this intellectually, but the body knows things the conceptual mind can't grok. My friend's feedback still hit me hard. Why, I wondered? Because this valid critique from a sharp and caring friend — as I took the implication — called into question the idea that I was indeed good at something. My friend's feedback called into question my long-sought status as a good listener. The implication was that I sometimes spoke for others instead of letting them speak for themselves. And I really, really wanted to be regarded as someone with good listening skills. Let me just tell you how much I want to listen.

This implied criticism struck a painful chord with me because it evoked an earlier version of my interdependent self, perhaps a collegiate version — a guy who was beginning to invest strongly in self-inquiry and was trying, in his own self-involved ways, to do right by others, but too often thought he had it all figured out. I had worked long and hard to learn to listen, to deeply hear and know people, to invite voices into shared spaces and amplify them whenever I could. And I still wasn't all that great at it.

Wait, I wanted to say defensively to my friend, I've been working on this tendency, really hard, for over twenty years! It's so confusing! I'm never sure whether to listen or speak! People are always asking for my opinion. They actually think I know something! And then suddenly I'm in a situation where the person wants me to shut up and hold space for them, and it's not always easy to read what's expected of me and to make that shift, you know? And by the way, what do I do with all the other feedback I've received from people of different embodiments that says something different from what you're saying now? How do I sort through all these differing perspectives on where my work lies?

But none of that response uttered aloud would've helped anyone, least of all myself. All those reactive thoughts were misdirected self-protection against personal ghosts. I had asked for, and received, the gift of a small bit of critical feedback, delivered with love, from a voice I respected. For once, I knew enough to breathe into the ouch, thank my colleague and friend for it, and contemplate what the feedback said about how I showed up in the community.

The Inner Critic Meets the Outer Critic

Why does the wind of criticism hurt so much? Why does it deflate us? Why do we spend so much of our lives defending against it? The old playground chant should go "Sticks and stones may break my bones (temporarily), but words will ruin my self-regard for lifetimes." Many of us didn't receive proper validation when we were younger. The way we showed up in the world was cut down while our sense of self was still developing, often by the people from whom we most needed positive support. Out of this early history came defensiveness and fragility about our perceived shortcomings, both practical ("You always leave crumbs on the kitchen counter!") and existential ("You, my dear, are a shitty friend"). Every once in a while when I say something that doesn't land well with my daughter, my inner dad critic wonders, *How many years of therapy and mindfulness practice will that moment cost her?*

Never mind criticism from other people; often the inner critic paralyzes us before we can even try and take our seats. Some of us have been left with inner critics so strategic and cunning that it can be the work of an entire lifetime to even become aware that the voice is overlaid on top of our lived experience, not the experience itself. To realize that the critic is just a *voice*, rather than an objective reality, is a massive step forward that deserves a great deal of, well, praise.

Inner criticism comes alive in our meditation practice, and confronting those voices is one of the most crucial reasons we practice meditation to begin with. Those inner Maras are a very tough crowd. If we're going to work with insecurity, we have to understand these voices and learn to work with, instead of against, their energy.

At the same time, there's the whole external world telling us our deal. As the saying goes, "Everyone's a critic." As we work with our inner critics, we have to simultaneously work with the prospects of criticism (and yes, praise) from others as well. In my example, my trusted friend was an external voice calling into question my listening skills at the same time that I felt internally fragile about my abilities in that department. That social piece of the puzzle greatly complicates the practice of working with criticism.

Most of us receive neither criticism nor compliments well. Why? Well, for one crucial reason, praise and blame operate on our nervous system in much the same way that pleasure and pain do. Evolutionary biology reminds us that praise and criticism, just like physical pleasure and pain, are meaningful because of the social nature of our survival. We are social creatures: we depend on relationships to survive. Praise or criticism are tied to our place in a group. Maybe the group is our family, maybe it's our school crew, maybe it's colleagues or the audience who benefits from our work. Maybe, in our crazy social media world, it's the public at large. Generally speaking, criticism makes our "seat" feel less safe within the defined community. We don't have to fear saber-toothed tigers in modern life, but we do worry about our reputation, because our standing in society is based on external opinions and perceptions. An attack to our reputational "self" can activate fear just as strongly as an attack on our physical body. Praise and affirmation, on the other hand, can make our place in the group feel reassured.

If you are present with the receipt of criticism, it can feel almost as primal and embodied as a cut, itch, or punch to the body. Your reputation is your true avatar, and its well-being is tied deeply to your sense of being okay.

As with pleasure and pain, there's a third sort of discomfort related to praise and criticism, which is the space in between the two. So often we face the discomfort of not knowing what someone thinks of us. When we don't know what others think of us, that uncertainty can cause as much stress and suffering as even the harshest criticism. This is why people say things like "You must *hate* me, don't you?" Even knowing we're hated can feel, oddly, more comforting than not knowing where we stand. At least criticism gives the ego some solid material to work with, something we can push back against, in order to feel solid ourselves. But with not knowing, we're back in that same sense of floating through outer space that we're so poorly equipped to face as humans.

I receive a lot of feedback. And for that reason, it has gotten much easier for me to practice receiving it. But it's still really hard. Like anything else, there's an "exposure therapy" component to praise and blame. I try to ask for feedback on whatever I'm doing. Even so, a lot of the feedback I get is, shall we say, unsolicited. I used to believe that if I held my seat with true confidence, eventually feedback simply wouldn't affect me anymore. But remember what happened when the Jedi of Mindfulness engaged in the pain experiment? While it lasted, Mingyur Rinpoche felt the sensation more fully as a result of his practice. We can never expect to feel unaffected by the forces of hope and fear, and that's true of praise and criticism as well. Because feedback doesn't — at first glance — seem physical in nature, we are more likely to misperceive it as something that exists only ephemerally and psychologically, and therefore, something we might eventually just get over.

We are socialized to view sensitivity to criticism, like pain, as a sort of weakness that needs to be conquered. I've come to believe that phrases like "Just let it roll off your back" or "Tune out the noise" aren't useful. For one thing, we can't do either of these when we're paying close attention. We are always perceiving and receiving. Even if the "noise" of feedback occurs at low volume, we still hear it. For another thing, tuning out doesn't allow us to make use of feedback, to use it to develop clarity and fine-tune our way of showing up. Instead, just as the pain experiment shows, we need try to hold our seats while cultivating greater sensitivity to the present moment. Fragility and sensitivity are two very different things. Sensitivity means feeling your response to the moment deeply and fully. Sensitivity means appreciating your humanity. Fragility means losing your seat, not being able to handle what you feel, and therefore reacting mindlessly. Instead of tuning out criticism, it's more useful to think of letting it move through you, feeling it while it's there, and making use of whatever information resonates. Easier said than done, but that's why we practice.

The Practice of Receiving Feedback

Over the years, based on practices of wise speech and deep listening, I've developed some guidelines for asking for and being open to feedback, especially as we navigate this technological era. If the ideas below are at all useful to you in working with the winds of praise and blame, please make use of them.

1. Prepare Yourself for the Ouch

Receiving feedback is always uncomfortable. Much of the discomfort originates in that neutral space in between positive and negative feedback, where we don't know what someone thinks of us. Even if you get feedback from someone who has nothing but great things to say about your qualities or your work, a person whose opinion you trust completely, you are still being beheld. The irony of feedback is that while we long to be known by others, it's also fundamentally uncomfortable to be seen. There's something inherently naked and tender about being assessed, even if you feel vulnerable for only a moment. Being witnessed by another person is just…awkward. Such is the nature of human connection and the nature of colliding subjectivities. The feeling of putting yourself — and your reputation — out into the world is always uneasy, even if you grow accustomed to receiving feedback. Returning to the rule of pleasure and pain: don't expect yourself to ever stop feeling.

As much as we'd like to pretend we could eventually float upward into an avoidant realm where feedback has no effect on us, it's just not possible. Ignoring its effects leads to a whole host of problems, like the insecure need for praise, passive aggression, or lashing out at others. Pretending we might one day get over praise and blame is silly, and there's often useful feedback in validation and criticism that can hone our skills and make us more grounded, effective, and compassionate.

"Preparing for the ouch" does not mean bracing unnecessarily or spinning out into cycles of rumination about how you might be perceived. It means that whenever you put yourself "out there" in some way, you prepare yourself by contemplating the basic view that when responses come back, they're probably going to make you feel something that's not entirely comfortable to feel. Praise generally feels good, but it can be overwhelming, just like pleasure. Criticism generally hurts, just like pain. Not knowing what others think can feel anchorless and uncomfortable. These facts of life aren't going to change, even if you become an awakened Buddha. Knowing that a feeling is coming, we can remind ourselves of the power of owning our humanity instead of trying to escape it.

2. Pause and Remember the Negativity Bias

It's amazing what happens when you receive feedback that contains even a molecule of criticism. I've watched my mind while receiving feedback about a course I'm teaching or a piece of writing. I might receive an email that raises ten different points about the work, and nine of them might be praise and validation. But eyes and ears will comb and scour, usually before I'm even aware it's happening, for the one piece that's negative. Like an archer focusing on a target, the mind goes straight to the critical piece before absorbing any of the validating information. It's humbling to watch the erasure of all praise, witnessing the mind sink its jagged teeth into the one piece of feedback that suggested we're not quite there yet.

Most of this internal one-sidedness is due to the negativity bias, the way our nervous systems have evolved to highlight potential threats and filter out other information. When receiving feedback, I try to remember that part of my mind always fears for my reputational survival, even if it's the most benign moment imaginable. Maybe I'm only asking my friend if they liked the salmon I just cooked. When I received that email feedback from my teaching colleague, I noticed my brain fixating on their mention of hearing the same thing from "multiple people." (*So, exactly how many people think I suck?*) That drew my attention away from the content of the feedback itself, which was useful to my development.

Therefore, whenever you can, remember to pause and breathe after the receipt of feedback. If you use practices like loving-kindness or self-compassion, take a few moments to do those practices. Try not to respond immediately (*yikes! not easy!*). Remembering that vulnerability is part of being human helps us to stay balanced and receptive when we're in the tender moment of being assessed. The reason feedback is so important to us is that it relates to our position in our group. When we pause, we're better able to absorb constructive aspects of the feedback rather than defending or deflecting.

The negativity bias causes another distortion in our relationship to praise and criticism: it causes us to overpersonalize everything. Even if you receive criticism about a behavior or piece of work that speaks clearly and effectively to the issue at hand without vilifying you as a human, the negativity bias can make you feel like you're being called a "bad self," who is under attack. For example, if your partner says, "I moved the clothes from the washer to the dryer this morning," that doesn't necessarily mean they're calling you a dumbass, even if you forgot to move it yourself. It just means an event happened that you needed to be told about. Since self is a fluid process, not a solid entity, looking for the "bad me" at the center of critical feedback is always going to be a fool's errand. In the pause, we allow ourselves to take a little longer and see how we're defending against a threat to our well-being that's most likely nonexistent.

3. *Know Who You're Asking for Feedback, and Why*

My friend Susan Piver — author, Buddhist teacher, and entrepreneur — once shared wonderful advice on how to seek feedback from others. She often works on long-term creative projects. She had one friend she would ask for feedback when she was at work on a project, but he would focus almost entirely on pointing out potential obstacles in the project, rather than seeing the imaginative opportunities of her work. She realized that this wasn't a helpful person to ask for feedback early on in her process. At that point, to feed her creativity and get the work rolling, she needed a "hype man," to put it in the eternal terms of hip-hop, not a grad school thesis adviser. If Susan only focused on obstacles before she got the work rolling, her inspiration would be hampered and the momentum of the project would be stalled. This particular friend's feedback was on point, so Susan always asked for it, but she'd request it later in the process, when the body of the work was already sturdy enough to incorporate the "glass is half empty" approach he brought. That way she could use his feedback to sharpen and refine the work like a scalpel, instead of halting her momentum like a roadblock.

When you're requesting feedback, it's nice to have multiple voices who can serve different roles in the way they assess you. First, make sure you have at least one or two "hype people" in your corner who raise you up no matter what, and who only care that you're trying. If hip-hop stars, who often seem like the most confident humans of all time, need hype men, then we all do. If hilarious comedians need someone to warm up the audience for them . . . you get the point. The story goes that the Buddha attained enlightenment in complete isolation (without any hype men), but as I grow older I believe this Ayn Rand–esque version of his story less and less. I think Siddhartha could spend so much time alone because he was tapping into a more cosmic lineage ancestry and support system. (I discuss that in the next section of the book.) I believe wisdom beings were reminding Siddhartha of his awakened potential every step of the way. If we are each going to hold our seat through all the criticism we receive for engaging wholeheartedly in the world, we need people in our corner showing us what the humanist psychologist Carl Rogers called "unconditional positive regard" — people who reflect back to us our inherent worthiness when we get stuck and just don't want to show up.

But if all you have is hype people, you're in trouble. If no one ever gives you difficult feedback, your being grows increasingly fragile, and you get addicted to the need for constant validation. This sort of echo chamber tends to develop in the leadership of spiritual communities when things go awry (as I know from experience). To balance out the hype people, I try to get feedback from multiple people who don't have the same vantage point on life — or on me. And I try to remember that asking for feedback puts the other person under no obligation to give it or to teach me anything.[1] When I sought feedback from my teaching colleague, the two of us were friends in the midst of an ongoing dialogue regarding what we all needed to reflect on during the difficult times we were sharing. We were mutually invested in each other's well-being. That feedback was freely given and received. It was a gift, and I tried to receive it in that spirit, without any expectations that my friend would help me learn what I needed to learn. How or whether I chose to act on the feedback was up to me. And, most important, don't

---

1 The comedian Sarah Cooper half-joked online during the summer of 2020, when Black Lives Matter was coming to a new international prominence, "It's exhausting being everyone's one Black friend right now."

ask somebody what they think unless you *really* want them to tell you.

Then there's the question of taking feedback from experts, those with hard-won knowledge and experience in their field. Experts are the elders who have more knowledge and experience than you or me. Guess what: some people know more than we do about whatever work we're engaged in. We're not all experts at everything, and that's a good thing! "Experts" have invested far more time practicing and studying. Experts willingly take on the job of teaching us something we don't already know and couldn't learn without help. And while experts always have their own subjective biases (every field of expertise develops its own institutional blind spots, and sometimes they are massive ones), experts can also build our confidence. We don't bow down to elders because they're better or smarter than us. We bow because they've been practicing a long time and have wisdom and knowledge from which we can learn.

Expertise needs to be respected, because without it, we're all just making it up, stumbling our way through the darkness. We could be willing to humble ourselves to look to the advice and guidance of those who know more than we do about the matter at hand. We shouldn't just be listening to the voices who tell us what we want to hear. That is an important lesson from the pandemic, when far too many people ignored the advice of nearly every public health expert and deemed themselves armchair epidemiologists with PhDs from YouTube University. But in the end, of course you have to trust yourself to employ the feedback you receive. If you don't trust yourself, then what do you have?

4. *Observe the Principal Witness: Working with Unsolicited Feedback*

There's a great slogan from classic Tibetan Buddhism on the bodhisattva path, the path of working with relationships in a compassionate way. It translates (slightly mysteriously) as "Of the two witnesses, observe the principal one." The two witnesses are yourself and others, and you are always the principal witness of your own actions and behaviors. The slogan means that we always have access to other people's opinions, and then we have our own insight and intuition into how we're doing and what path we need to pursue. This is true of any situation where we are trying to make something happen, whether it's starting a new organization, being in a romantic relationship, or pursuing spiritual awakening.

If we're wise, we seek the counsel of others, especially wise friends and elders. But we're also going to get feedback from those whose opinion we never asked. Often, unsolicited feedback comes from those who are uninvested in the work you're doing or have motives other than a genuine care for your progress as a human. You may even be told what's wrong with you by people who are confusing you with someone else. People frequently give unsolicited feedback in their most reactive moments.

Our technology not only allows this reactive feedback but tends to encourage it. We each receive feedback that is wildly projective and just plain off. There is an interesting kind of feedback that's become immensely popular, a style of discourse that's simultaneously totally disinterested yet shockingly intense. This is the sort of "gotcha" feedback, most common on social media, where the main intention is to dunk on people, not to help anyone. It's amazing how much time people spend commenting on things they don't really know or care about. This is most definitely the era of hot takes.

Just as technology has fundamentally altered our relationship to pleasure and pain, it has also taken the task of working with praise and criticism into a tornado zone of misinformation, zingers, dunks, and bad takes. We're all struggling with how to become more mature in listening and expressing ourselves. This struggle would still be happening if all we had were our face-to-face exchanges with the people in our immediate social circles. Giving and receiving feedback is hard enough between people who know and trust one another. Now, it's almost as if social media companies are saying to us: "Having trouble learning how to listen fully and speak genuinely with the people in your life? How about trying it with thousands of strangers, simultaneously?"

The usefulness of technology to help us hear and see more perspectives directly mirrors its potential to undercut our confidence. Like many people, I've spent time licking my wounds because somebody sent me a harsh email about my work or a mean comment on a social media post. When that happens, I try to practice compassion for myself and for that person (except when it's a bot, because you can practice compassion only for sentient beings). I try to remember that I'm still learning how to express myself effectively, and that all us humans are just learning how to talk to each other. In the immortal words of the Digable Planets: "We're just babies, man." But unsolicited feedback, especially in algorithmically driven social media pile-ons, can also be harmful, activating us in ways that undercut both our confidence and our ability to hear and incorporate any of the wisdom the feedback might contain. For some of us, unsolicited feedback can even become physically dangerous.

My friend Shannon Watts is a Buddhist practitioner and activist who started a hugely successful grassroots movement called Moms Demand, which pressures lawmakers to pass more sensible gun laws across the United States, a country with more civilian-held guns than there are humans to hold them.[2] As a result, over the past decade, Shannon has experienced death threats, doxxing, and terrifying treatment from the National Rifle Association and people online who simultaneously hate her and love guns. I asked her how she works with receiving this hate on her large social media platform. She said, "While it may be tempting to fire back at trolls, as Glennon Doyle once said, "'There are not two of you — Internet You and Real You. There is only one of you. If you aren't kind on the internet, then you're not kind.'" Shannon also said, "I've blocked so many people on Twitter that the hashtag #ImBlockedByShannonWatts once trended. I also report users (although, truthfully, this is less effective now given Twitter's new owner, Elon Musk). By reporting social media guideline offenders, you protect yourself and you make social media platforms safer spaces for everyone. Finally, never engage in personal attacks, and stick to subjects you truly understand."

I've been asked if it was okay to be Buddhist and block people on social media. There are — obviously — no classic teachings on this matter, but here is my opinion. If someone repeatedly makes personal attacks on you or others, rather than engaging with what you have to say in a way that makes you

---

2 The United States has almost three times as many civilian-owned guns per capita as the country ranking second, which is Yemen.

believe they're genuinely interested in a respectful exchange — and certainly if someone threatens you personally — you need to block them and feel assured that it's the compassionate thing to do.

Not all unsolicited feedback is trolling, and some of it can be useful. I've gotten some great feedback from people I never asked and didn't know. My guideline for incorporating unsolicited feedback is to always do my best to listen and see if the person is coming from positive intentions. I've learned so much from opening my eyes and ears to the things people are saying. The multiplicity of perspectives is the saving grace of our online spaces. If a person says something that doesn't resonate with my inner compass (the principal witness), I thank them and move on. But if I start to hear the same thing from multiple sources, and it resonates (partially or fully) with me, I do my best to contemplate and integrate what they're saying into my behavior over time.

5. *Squirm and Take That Compliment*

What about getting praise? You know, when someone tells you what you're doing is awesome? You know that feeling, right? I hope you do. Praise is not only validating, it's essential for accessing your confidence. Praise reminds you that effort pays off and reinforces a sense of worthiness. We each need other people to tell us we're basically good, that we matter, that we're amazing in our own way, and most importantly, that we're headed in the right direction for growth to occur. We all need people who appreciate us and remind us that all the hard work of taking our seat is worthwhile. Praise also reminds you of all the things you *don't* need to work on. Much of the time, our desire not to mess up will lead us to focus on the things we already do well, when we really need to lean into the places where we feel less secure. If we lean too hard on our strengths, we end up lopsided.

Sure, some of us have an addictive relationship to praise that mirrors an addictive relationship to pleasure. But most people I know grow visibly uncomfortable when they come face to face with genuine praise. If you want to see a person squirm, find somebody you care about right now and give them a compliment for no reason. Watch that person try to change the subject or look at you like you're high. As much as the winds of criticism can hurt, the receipt of appreciation makes us feel equally naked and vulnerable. In the same way that it's hard to be fully and completely present with a moment of pleasure, it's difficult to hold your seat through a moment of praise. Personally, when I receive praise, it can feel overwhelming in my body. I find myself deflecting or instantly talking about all the many other people I need to give credit. When a student or someone I mentor compliments me, I often find myself wondering if the compliment is the person projecting their own good qualities and results of their hard work onto me (often, yes, they are doing just that). This response is a reasonable defense mechanism against future pain because positive projections can turn out to be just as dangerous as negative projections, especially when the person's projections are disappointed later on. For every pedestal that someone puts you on, there's an opportunity to be cut down in the future. And if they're putting you on a spiritual pedestal, then their eventual disappointment with you can be that much greater.

Still, just as we have to learn to feel the ouch of criticism more fully, we also have to learn to feel the gooey, chocolate-all-over-your-face warmth of praise as well. We have to practice holding our seats with both of these winds. So the next time someone compliments you, see if you can pause for a moment. Notice any tendency to ignore, deflect, or explain away the praise. Stay with your body instead. And simply practice saying these two words: "Thank you."

The Practice of Giving Feedback

Because praise and criticism happen in the interpersonal realm, we can create these forces in another person's experience just as much as we can experience them ourselves. How you give feedback is just as important as how you receive it. When the roles reverse, here are some guidelines I try my best to practice.

1. Question Whether the Feedback Is Helpful Coming from You

My great-uncle Irv, who was considered a bodhisattva-mensch among the Jewish half of my family, supposedly said, "Don't ever tell anyone anything unless they have a place to put it." Whether or not a person is positioned to receive your feedback depends on trust and timing. We need to ask ourselves, Is this the right time, and am I the right person? Did they ask me for my opinion? What is my position relative to this person? Do I have credibility with them? Do they trust me? Does the situation at hand actually involve me? Am I giving feedback just to exert some form of righteous power over them? Can I offer this feedback in a way that they will hear? Do they have a place to put my feedback right now?

When I look in the mirror, I see a goofball. But people I work with don't always see me that way, and I have to be aware of my role. Once the Dalai Lama advised an elderly monk not to do certain Buddhist practices that were physical and based in yogic principles, because they took a very long time and were best done when a practitioner was younger. The monk supposedly misinterpreted this advice to mean that if he was reborn in a younger body, he would be able to do this set of practices. So he committed suicide.[3] Now, the Dalai Lama could never have anticipated that his words could be misinterpreted so badly. He had probably talked to hundreds of people asking for his feedback that day alone. He wasn't responsible for the suicide. But still, our feedback matters to other people, and if we don't contemplate our position in someone's life, we can cause great distress. If you want to tell someone something you think they need to hear, take a moment to contemplate your relationship with this person before proceeding.

Of course, if you are giving feedback that involves your own needs, you may choose to do so regardless of whether the other person "wants" to hear it from you. If you need to quit your job or tell a friend that their actions hurt you, you're the only one who can give that feedback, and there's always a chance the other person might not take it well. And if that happens, you may have to make a tough decision and set a boundary in your relationship with them. Most of the time, if you set a personal boundary with someone and they react by attacking

3 This story appears in *The Art of Happiness* and is revisited in Pema Chödrön's *Getting Unstuck*.

or demanding more of you, it simply validates that setting a boundary with them — at least for now — was the right thing to do.

Sometimes we need to say something, sometimes we need to ask someone else to say something for us, and sometimes we need to set a boundary and let the other person know we're not available for them right now. In these cases, it's right to think more about whether giving the feedback is important for you, rather than speculating on what the other person might do with it.

2. *Speak to Behaviors and Impacts, Not Identities and Intentions*

It's important to remember the basic Buddhist view that there isn't a solid self. Each person is the amalgam of many causes. The person you're addressing doesn't have a single unchanging being. Just like you, this person is dynamic and complex. This person may manifest differently in different life situations, and you only experience some of their actions and the impacts of those actions upon you. You're also not the only individual experiencing them, and you can't speak for everyone. You're a subjective being, interacting with another subjective being. We can't know another person's internal landscape or their intentions (although it may be helpful to ask questions about where they were coming from or what they were trying to do in the situation under discussion). Regardless of a person's intent, however, we can address the felt impact of their actions. The more you know a person and the more they trust you, the easier it becomes to generalize feedback ("One thing I've noticed about you the last several years . . ."), but even then, there can be a danger in trying to depict the trends you see in a globalized manner. The most useful feedback draws on specific examples and articulates how the action or situation has affected us, which gives the recipient tools to understand it from another perspective.

3. Remember the Ouch and the Negativity Bias, and Speak Appreciatively

You may say nine positive things and make one criticism. But the negativity bias baked into the human nervous system means the criticism will be heard more loudly than the praise. We can't do too much about this feature of our design other than to reinforce a basic sense of positivity when we say what we have to say.

I've found it's also important to push back against the tendency to hide behind technology and try to rely on the written word as little as possible in having potentially difficult conversations. This feels most true in situations where mutual trust hasn't been earned, or when trust has been ruptured in some way. Tone of voice and body language carry much more emotional connection than text messages. Online comments have even worse issues: they can be easily manipulated by algorithms, and they turn a private conversation into a public one, which pressures all participants to perform a response, rather than relate authentically to one another as humans.

Of course, you're always free to tell somebody what their deal is using language that is entirely negative, overly harsh, full of generic, personal attacks, and without showing any interest in their own development. This sort of "dunking" speech may give you an exhilarating feeling of playground superiority for a moment, but it usually ends up leaving both parties feeling undercut and less confident than before. If you haven't already tried this approach a thousand times (I have), then go for it, and pay close attention to how you feel after the initial high of the "dunk" wears off.

4. Let Go of Results

The same contemplative slogans from the eleventh century that tell us to trust our own witness above all else also contain this gem: "Abandon any hope of results." This slogan tells us that we can't control the outcomes of our actions. Abandoning hope of results is a great idea to keep in your back pocket whenever giving feedback to another person. With mindfulness, we can learn to exercise a good deal of clarity over how we offer feedback, and this alone is empowering. But we have very little control regarding how that feedback is received. We have even less (read: absolutely no) control over what the person does with that feedback.

The other person might have begged you to share your thoughts. You might be in the perfect trusting relationship to tell the flawed yet beautiful human in front of you exactly what you see. You might speak insightfully to their actions and tendencies without overpersonalizing or attacking them. You might express your words appreciatively, positioning any criticism within a genuine hopefulness that what you share will simply help their positive qualities grow more and more. And still you might miss the mark. You might raise all their defenses, hurt them deeply, or just piss them off. This is a risk we take every time we share feedback.

Even worse, the person might agree with you completely in

the moment, nodding excitingly and saying "I know, you're *so* right, I know exactly what you mean!" And then they do precisely zero to integrate your feedback into their daily life. Isn't that our coolest defense mechanism — agreeing completely with what another person suggests, and then acting on absolutely none of what they say? Mentors, teachers, and therapists know this strategy well. Fun times.

If the feedback isn't well received, or isn't used, there's not much you can do. Personal transformation can take a whole lifetime, if not multiple lifetimes, and it never happens just because one wise person said one perfectly compassionate thing at just the right moment. I have spent much of my own life wishing a wisdom holder would just give me the "eureka" secrets of what I'm doing right or wrong. It doesn't work that way. We don't live inside a fortune cookie. Change is slow. By abandoning hope of results when we offer (and, for that matter, receive) feedback, we can acknowledge that wanting to help a person may turn into wanting to rescue them from their own confusion. Watching someone suffer or cause harm is painful — especially if you believe the other person is in danger — but if you decide to offer feedback about their situation, you also have to let them figure out for themselves what, if anything, they're willing to do about it.

Like pleasure and pain, praise and criticism are experiences that don't stop with the physical body. They extend to our sense of who we are, to our relationships, and to the groups in which we all seek acceptance and validation. Remembering your inherent sensitivity as a human, you can take your seat more mindfully and attend to receiving and giving feedback with the care and attention it deserves.

CHAPTER FOUR

Influence and Insignificance

Avoiding the Second Death

> *She's got 34,000 Instagram followers. There were three people at her birthday party.*
>
> — Overheard New York (Instagram Feed)

A Disney movie took my understanding of the truth of impermanence to a whole new level. The movie *Coco* introduces the idea that a person dies twice. The plot revolves around the Mexican holiday El Día de los Muertos. It follows the twelve-year-old musician Miguel into La Tierra de los Muertos (Land of the Dead), to meet his great-great-grandfather and discover the ancestral origins of the reason why members of his family are now forbidden to play music. *Coco*'s a real tearjerker (Pixar is brilliant at the feat of emotional manipulation).

In Miguelito's journey we find out that a person's death occurs not just once, but twice. When the body dies, a spirit moves from the land of the living to the land of the dead, but this death is not the final one. The second death — the final death — happens when none of your descendants in the land of the living remembers you well enough to make an *ofrenda* (offering) for you on their familial altar. When all memories of you fade from the living, that's when you're done. Your spirit dissolves into a psychedelic layer of *cempasúchil* flowers, and you're gone.

The third pair of hope and fear has everything to do with avoiding this second death, the death of being *known*. The winds of influence and insignificance point to a longing to be recognized, to gain visibility and fame in the world, and to avoid obscurity and unimportance. In some Buddhist translations, the negative wind in this duo is translated as *infamy*. But in this age where being famous in any form often "trumps" whether or not you're known for good things, antiheroes are just as capable of building their platforms and harvesting power and riches as those who are known for good works and heroic deeds. Some people even prefer to be antiheroes, living in infamy, as a way to leverage their power and build renown for their rebelliousness. These days, as long as people are watching you, it doesn't always matter whether they like you. You can get famous for being disliked by the same people your followers dislike. Infamy can be monetized.[1] For that reason, I prefer the term *insignificance* — being forgotten completely.

It's possible that influence and insignificance don't seem as important to you as the winds we've already discussed. Not everybody cares about being widely known. The longing for

---

1 In her amazing book *Doppelganger*, Naomi Klein delves deeply into the process of becoming infamous as she watches a formerly progressive and feminist author, Naomi Wolf (someone with whom Klein has frequently been confused), veer to the world of alt-right politics, promoting conspiracy theories and gaining a new and different sort of alternative fame for doing so.

recognition is something with which I've had a complex relationship. Perhaps the reason I wanted to be a writer was because — if I became known — it'd be the sort of notoriety where people know your work but not your face. Anonymous fame sounded — and still sounds — ideal to me. I never saw myself as becoming known as a spiritual teacher. That recognition brought with it all sorts of odd projections by others about who I was — or, more accurately, who I was supposed to be. These assumptions about me — mostly false — wouldn't have been useful for the people I worked with had they been true. I spend most days of my life attempting to dismantle these assumptions and be a decent, flawed human making gradual progress on his journey of awakening. Occasionally, when I meet someone who has heard me speak, read my books, or connected with my work, before I can even say a word, they dive into telling me how guilty they feel because their meditation practice has fallen off recently. I just want to ask them how life is going, yet all of a sudden here we are, at a random restaurant in a city I'm visiting, or on a rush-hour subway platform transformed into an impromptu mindfulness confessional. I most definitely never signed up to be a priest.

One time I was out to dinner with my friend and teacher Sharon Salzberg, who is renowned in the mindfulness world for good reason. The waitress recognized Sharon. She had listened to Sharon's audiobooks and guided meditations, and she definitely "fangirled" a bit when she saw Sharon sit down to eat. The waitress very pleasantly described how she listened to Sharon's talks and guided meditations and how they were helping her a lot with both anxiety and getting to sleep at night. "Have you ever thought about just how many people listen to your voice?" the waitress asked, semi-rhetorically. "Have you ever thought about how many people listen to your voice...in bed?" I couldn't help but giggle at that particular turn of phrase. Sharon thought the whole thing was sweet.

Regardless of whether you seek fame, we all have complex relationships with our own visibility, and most of the structures of our current technology weaponize that complexity. For the first time in history, a person can keep statistical track of how many people are following and liking their public — and private — activities. Kids my daughter's age have their own YouTube channels — low-budget reality TV shows for the younger set — with millions of subscribers, generating revenue that supports and enriches their whole family. In his book *The Craving Mind*, Dr. Judson Brewer cites research that links time spent on social media with heightened activity in the nucleus accumbens, a region of the brain involved in the experience of social reward, including positive recognition from others. Getting likes and followers not only increases your public visibility; it can also change your brain in measurable ways.

The ability to earn a living is now often related to the reach of a person's social media presence or "platform." When a book publisher considers publishing your work, they don't just decide whether it's good enough to be published on its merits (although that's a part of the process). They want to know many details of your platform: how many followers you have, how many subscribers are on your email list, and what connections you can leverage to get the book you're writing in front of maximum readers. This all makes financial sense. When you're introducing a new product, you want to know there's already an audience for said product. Having an existing audience and platform is necessary for success in many other creative fields as well. Recognition is useful. But when the cultivation of your "audience" is happening separately from doing the work that might meritoriously earn you that audience, we find ourselves in this new terrain of "influencers." Sadly, the need to leverage a platform affects the world of wellness and mindfulness in increasingly perverse ways.

Whenever I hear the term *mindfulness influencer*, I laugh and cringe at the same time. What, exactly, is an influencer? The original human to claim this term was most likely Paris Hilton, an heiress who became increasingly known in the late 1990s and early 2000s for being seen at parties and attracting media attention just for her attendance. Her renown was derived from, well, itself. She got famous for being famous, which she then spun into more fame. Others, including the billionaire Kardashians as well as the first (and hopefully only) reality-TV president in US history, followed in her footsteps. Getting famous for being famous has become a perfectly samsaric feedback loop.

You'll Only Be Canceled by Death, and That's for Sure

I hesitate to use the term *canceled* to describe our fear of insignificance. The expression is a trope of fearmongering that distracts us — as almost all fearmongering does — from the real issue regarding what behaviors we're accountable for when we have power, as well as how power is fairly distributed in communities and society. In reality, nobody is ever canceled in the sense of ceasing to exist in the public sphere: they've just lost the consent of whatever audience they had. People who were voluntarily following them have now decided not to support them anymore. Fans are never promised to any of us. We can ask valid questions about whether certain mistakes warrant immediate judgment of a person's humanity, but that's a different topic, which requires us to reflect on the role of punishment in healing and justice. When discussing the hope for recognition, we need to remember that no one is *owed* fame. To give someone attention is an act of choice, and it's not a permanent choice. And the loss of this attention rarely causes true damage. Perhaps there are a few cases where deep and lasting harm has been caused to a person who suddenly lost their job or their position for misspeaking or making a relatively small mistake. But for the most part, those who have been canceled are doing just fine. In fact, many of those who shout the loudest about having been canceled now have a larger following than ever.[2]

Still, the *fear* of cancellation is very real, and it's tied into the primal fear of becoming insignificant to, or an outcast from, your group. Again, hope and fear are always real feelings worthy of respect, even if the *experiences* that our hopes and fears point toward are often exaggerated, or even mirages. The fear of cancellation reflects the valid anxiety about doing something that can't be healed or repaired. This is part of the reason why the term *cancel culture* caught on so widely. I certainly know the fear of saying or doing the wrong thing publicly or

---

2 While recently listening to a podcast conversation between Joe Rogan and Elon Musk (I try to listen to those with whom I disagree), both men voiced dismay at their own "cancellation." If the richest human and the most popular podcaster on the planet can both refer to themselves using this term, then clearly it has departed from its original meaning of losing power and fame entirely.

privately, of causing harm when I didn't mean to. As individuals in personal relationships, we do often cancel each other, as when we shut someone out and give up on them completely because of a blind spot revealed, a harm caused, or a mistake made. We've inherited the view that justice has to be punitive in order to maintain the social order. Make a mistake, pay the price. When it comes to the public eye, the structures of media and social media greatly intensify this fear.

Most of us long for recognition from others in one form or another. And if we happen to get some recognition or renown, we ought to remember that, just like any other experience, being in the spotlight is an experience bounded by impermanence. It can't and won't last.

It's worth contemplating the two forms of death that *Coco* brings to our attention. There's no way to say this, except straightforwardly: not only will we all die — a truth that requires tremendous self-compassion to even begin to contemplate — but there will be a time on this earth when nobody will know that we even existed. In the end, the cosmos is laughing at every last one of us. What an ouch! Even if you turned out to be one of the very rare people whose "brand" survives for thousands of years, you'd almost definitely be misremembered. There's no way world leaders from millennia ago like Zenobia or Alexander the Great lived exactly the lives that they are recorded as having lived. Siddhartha Gautama and Jesus Christ have showed unbelievable staying power in the fame of their spiritual stories, but those stories are almost certainly misrecorded and quite frequently misinterpreted. Jesus doesn't even get to be remembered as the race or ethnicity that he was in real life! And the dominant history of the United States itself is as much a PR campaign as anything else. Whatever people know us as, whatever they respect or resent us for, that remembrance will change, fade, and dissolve. My body will die, and all memory of me will die as well.

Aloneness

Sit quietly if you can. Take a few moments to consider what's it like to be alive when nobody is watching you. When there's no way to track how many other people are thinking about you — texting you, calling you, knocking on your door, making plans with you, following you online, hearing you, engaging with what you've created, "liking" or "disliking" your insights and achievements — how do your body and mind feel then? What's it like when no friends are around, or your kids aren't calling as much as you would like them to? If you have a partner, when they leave town for a week, how does that empty bed feel? (I'll admit, the first night usually feels pretty good.) If you're single, how does that status feel right now? (Likewise, I'll admit, the first few nights feel pretty good.) How does it feel to stop swiping right and left for a moment? If you long to be seen and known, does that longing come from a wish to share your life with others, or does it come from a fear of being erased or unseen? If it's a little of both (most likely), then how do those two forces coexist within you? How do you feel when you contemplate the second death, the end of being known in this world?

There are no right answers to any contemplative questions, especially these. The important part of any contemplation is keeping a given question in mind — in this case, the question of how it feels to be alone with ourselves. This is the best way

I've found to work with the forces of hope and fear related to my inevitable insignificance. For me, contemplating aloneness conjures a deep sadness and nostalgia. It brings to my heart the evaporation of a thousand perceived opportunities to share something of myself in a way that has meaning and impact, a thousand lost connections with others. But that sadness is also mixed with a sense of freedom and ease, that touch of humor that comes from not taking myself so seriously, of being fully sufficient in my own emotional experience. For me, the second death is both sad and liberating. It's not one and it's not the other. Emotions tend to be more of a "both-and" situation, not an "either/or" binary. Feeling the simultaneous sadness and liberation of my aloneness is perhaps the most important "both-and" feeling I know.

One of the main reasons we meditate is to accustom ourselves to this truth. This doesn't mean we don't connect deeply and intimately with others. It doesn't exclude intimacy; rather, befriending aloneness is the gateway to real connection. One of the most painfully beautiful things about going on a meditation retreat — even if it's only for a weekend — is the process of turning off from the world, putting all of your ways of witnessing and being witnessed by others out of sight for a period of time. You come back home having put in all this time working with your internal spaces, imagining how you might describe the subtle shifts in your experience to someone who wasn't part of the retreat. Because you're just so certain that *everyone* is going to want to hear about your experience! You hoist your bags, partially hoping there will be a celebration on your block when you return. Alas, no parade, no block party, no cookout. The world kept on doing its thing. The bizarre modern news cycle continued at its breakneck pace without you. People lived their lives. Those closest to you may want to hear what you experienced, and you may struggle to find the words. You may've hoped for the world to scream, "We missed you!" Instead, it's usually more like "Oh, you were gone?" And, let's be honest, "You were gone?" is only a very small step away from the world sighing limply "You're still here?" There's no better way to work with impermanence than to contemplate the truth of death. And there's no better preparation for the second death than going on — and returning from — a retreat.

What Do I Want to Be Known For?

Here's an interesting statistic about fame: Gallup approval ratings are done not only for political figures, but also for public figures. Two years before his death, in 1966, Dr. Martin Luther King Jr.'s approval rating among Americans was only 32 percent. His Gallup poll rating was never very high during his lifetime; it maxed out in the low 40s after the 1963 March on Washington, then fell as he began increasingly arguing for the economic redistribution of resources. In fact, Dr. King's Gallup approval during the later years of his life was actually two points lower than the lowest approval Donald Trump ever recorded during his presidency (Trump's Gallup poll rating bottomed out at 34 percent in the very last days of his administration, after he attempted to overthrow the US government on January 6, 2021). Dr. King in 1966 was less popular than President Donald Trump at his least popular moment.[3] Which one of the two would you rather be like?

---

3 In 2011, Dr. King's Gallup poll rating had shot up to 94 percent.

I've always had a conflicted relationship to seeking renown for myself. I'm old enough now to admit that I'm not super comfortable being beheld by groups of other people, even if it's a small group. But I do like being known for my work, as recognition both allows me to feel the validation of my inherent human worthiness and to feel useful and significant to others while I'm here. My first adult attempt to put myself out there and read my writing in front of others — at a poetry and performance series that a friend of mine put together — almost led to a panic attack. I made it through the reading with my legs shaking uncontrollably in front of a packed room of about 150 people at the Bowery Poetry Club. The friend who had organized the event laughed with — and at — me after the reading. Eventually I learned some helpful methods for feeling comfortable when speaking in front of others, and I've learned to hold my seat by doing it again and again thousands of times. (The practice of windhorse, which I describe in chapter 9, is one of these techniques.) But to this day, being in front of others requires me to engage in some contemplative practice and some other social tricks to break my own ice and relax into being beheld by others at the front of the room. After getting enough messages from people who told me I was decent at teaching, I decided that I was going to try to teach Buddhism for a living. I realized that I would need a platform to do this — a decision that automatically puts you into the windy arena of hoping for recognition and fearing insignificance.

Being Buddhist adds an additional layer of complexity to any activity that draws public attention. If you're an actor, people expect you to seek attention. If you're a Buddhist teacher, though, you might get judged by others for even looking like you *might* be seeking attention for yourself. When I started teaching outside my original Buddhist community (Shambhala) to try to link up with new audiences and forge new connections, I started a podcast (this was in the mid-aughties, way back before everyone had a podcast) and decided to write a book. Some people in my Buddhist community looked at me suspiciously, as if the act of using my voice was inherently egocentric and resoundingly arrogant. I'm not exaggerating. I received many emails from people wondering who had given me permission (or "blessings," as we say when we're feeling spiritual) to make these public-facing efforts, even though I had completed multiple teacher training programs and had dotted all the i's and crossed all the t's for doing what I was doing. The external Dharma Police (not to mention the voices in my head) were out in full force.

Meanwhile, when I submitted my first book proposal to my agent, she told me the exact opposite. I was way too humble, and I needed to learn how to promote myself much more. I was torn. Did I seek recognition too much or too little? If I hadn't had a few "hype people" in my life, and the willingness to put myself out there and make mistakes that comes in part from my privileged position in the world, I probably would have given up teaching early on. There was almost no money in it then, and there were myriad ways to fail, both economically and psychologically. These obstacles lead a lot of people to give up on teaching, which is why I now try to help newer teachers — Buddhist and otherwise — find their seats and learn to help others navigate their paths.

Now, a few decades later, have I made peace with being seen and known? That's like asking if the wind has stopped blowing, or if my inner tube man has been surgically removed. The winds do not cease, even if some days are stiller than others. I've made better friends with the process. My legs don't shake uncontrollably anymore, at least.

Contemplating Aloneness and Influence

Here are a few questions to keep in mind about having a platform and working with the winds of fame and insignificance. They are framed around the ideas of aloneness and influence. You might just want to sit and breathe in meditation posture before reflecting on these questions. They're just primers. Other questions may arise while contemplating these, and the key to any contemplation is to follow it wherever it goes. If journaling is your thing, you can always write down any images, reactions, emotions, or notes that come up as you contemplate these questions.

1. **Contemplate aloneness.** How does it feel in those times when no one's eyes are on you, when you feel unseen or uncredited? If you think about the second death, the end of your reputation in the world, how does that sit with you? How can remembering the second death be helpful to your work in this world?
2. **Contemplate the meaning of influence.** If I gain influence — in my family, my community, or my work — how do I want to use that influence? Am I in it just to make money? Do I need a lot of people to know me in order to feel significant? How can I acknowledge and credit the people who have helped me? How can

> I use whatever resources or renown I might acquire to amplify, mentor, and lift up the work of others? Can I create conditions where the influence I gain helps others to gain recognition and be of benefit to themselves and others?

Knowing that we live in the era of reality TV and influencers, where reputation and influence often take precedence over hard work and compassionate intention, it's important to contemplate how you might take your seat with intention and use whatever recognition comes your way to amplify compassion and wisdom in this world.

Coco ends with a contemplation of the kind of recognition that really matters. Miguel learns that his disgraced great-great-grandfather was himself a musician who died trying to get back to his family, and who wrote many well-known songs that another musician stole from him in order to increase his own fame. In the land of the living, as well as the land of the dead, Miguel is able to reunite the various generations of his family and start out on his own path as a musician. His story reminds us that those who do the hardest work frequently go without recognition. It also reminds us that it might be better to be known by a few loved ones than by thousands of fans. As you contemplate the winds of fame and insignificance, think about the sorts of recognition that truly matter to you. Exploring this pairing of hope and fear is also an opportunity to consider what influences we would like to have left behind when those first and second deaths come for us.

CHAPTER FIVE

Success and Failure

The Misery of Comparative Mind

HERE'S A FEELING A BUDDHIST GUY — or anyone else, probably — doesn't like to admit having: envy.

I've wanted to be a writer since seventh grade, when I had one of those amazing teachers who encourages you, inspires you, and challenges you.[1] Almost instantly writing became my main method for harmonizing an exchange with reality, learning to balance what I was receiving from the world with what I was expressing back to it. I knew at age twelve I was going to be a writer, even before I knew I was going to be a Buddhist. It wasn't until my mid-twenties that a harsh truth landed on my shoulders — an economic fact that no one bothers to tell you straightforwardly in the age of late capitalism, instead waiting for you to discover it when you look at your bank statement as a young adult. Almost no one gets to succeed as a writer (or any sort of artist, really) — at least not for a reliable paycheck, not saying exactly the things you wanted to say and having them reach the folks you imagined you'd reach. Most people who

1 Shout-out to Carol O'Donnell at the Manhattan Country School!

write never get published, and even those who see their work elevated into print, have to interweave that passion with other pursuits to make ends meet. But regardless of the near impossibility of making writing my career, through high school, college, and my mid-twenties, poetry and fiction were my first and second loves.

I went to college with a writer named Ben Lerner, who was a preternatural talent.[2] We weren't that close, but we were friendly and part of the same larger circle of friends. After college, I followed his work. Occasionally I'd email him to offer praise and say hi. Meanwhile, I was advancing on my Buddhist path and starting to teach. I wrote my first nonfiction book — about Buddhism and interdependence — for a small publisher. Buddhism wasn't exactly what I had always wanted to write about, but the book was generally well received. A number of years went by, and my reputation as a teacher grew — something that I never had on my grown-person bingo card. Over time, I became a medium-sized fish in the small pond of Western Buddhism. Meanwhile I self-published, as a labor of love with little fanfare, some fiction and poetry. Then I was approached by a young editor who had attended a number of my classes and worked for the prestigious publisher FSG, which also happened to be publishing Ben's acclaimed novel *10:04*.[3] My book *The Road Home* came from that collaboration with that awesome editor.[4] My literary friends were impressed I had landed such a prestigious publisher. My writing was progressing

2 I toyed with the idea of writing about Ben anonymously, but I figured, why not give the person whose work I respect and admire a shout-out?

3 Ben's next novel, *The Topeka School*, was a finalist for the Pulitzer Prize.

4 Thanks, Gabriella Doob.

and evolving. *The Road Home* was well received, and I knew it was a much more mature book than my first. *The Road Home* even landed, surprisingly, on a couple of lists for the best books of 2015.

Still, some undefined hint of adolescent disappointment with my grown-up seat in this world lingered on. Bubbles of recurrent thought would visit me, whispering that I hadn't done what I'd always longed to do, what I was *here* to do. It was an inexpressible nagging sensation of a partial failure, or at best an incomplete success. When it came to my writing, a piece of me was always chasing that mythical creature called confidence. My beloved editor left FSG right before my book was published. With her gone and my book's sales far below the threshold of a bestseller, I had no idea whether they would work with me on future projects.

Given that uncertainty, the morning FSG agreed to publish a second book of mine — especially the quirky combination of pop culture homage, memoir, and Buddhist take on modern relationships that I proposed — was a strong affirmation, to say the least. I got off the phone with my agent and had one of those "Mama, I made it!" moments. In fact, I did call my mother. My inner tube man was shooting upward, headwinds abounding, reanimating me. I was a writer. The identity I'd sought since seventh grade was verified, a little blue checkmark from the galaxy. Most writers would kill for what I had. I was getting paid a decent advance from a prestigious publisher — not enough to pay the bills, but the largest advance I had received, anyway — and some people I didn't even know were reading what I wrote. I could arrive at a feeling of settledness, safely rooted to this earth, not needing any more confirmation from the witnessing eyes of the world. Take my seat? *Check*. Confidence? *You know it, baby!* Equanimity? *It's my middle name.* My body was humming too strongly to meditate. The seemingly endless to-do list had faded into momentary irrelevance. After I told my mother the news, I turned off my phone and wandered around my native city for a few glorious hours. I'd tell everyone else later on. I had no agenda, nothing left to prove.

A few hours later I turned my phone back on. My phone dinged news notifications. The first one told me that Ben Lerner had been awarded a MacArthur Foundation "genius" grant, one of the highest honors, well, anywhere. Basically, you get a lot of money for the work you've already put in and get the galactically verified title of Genius.

I would like to say that my initial (internal) reaction to the news was magnanimous joy for a friend whose work I both respect and admire, but it wasn't. It was an oddly embarrassing feeling of deflation. My inner tube man went limp. My shoulders curled inward, as if my own moment of validation earlier in the day had happened to another person in another lifetime.

Don't worry: I recovered from this silly moment, and nobody would even know it had happened if it hadn't quickly become my favorite personal story about the insidious frenemy that Buddhists call "comparative mind." A secretly envious, late–Gen X spiritual teacher is the sort of deliciously postmodern character Ben Lerner himself might create. I share this story because it's tender, and we don't talk about the experience of comparative mind nearly enough. In recent years, much psychological and spiritual attention has been given to anxiety, anger, and addictive desire. Jealousy and envy remain in the shadows of our spiritual dialogue. Yet if recent history has taught us anything, it's that whatever remains hidden can cause huge problems if it's not brought into the light. Unacknowledged envy can make our actions self-involved, myopic, and fragile. Collectively experienced, comparison — our odd need to compete rather than collaborate — is a toxic trait that prevents us from creating a world where we delight in helping others get their basic needs met.

That day — that day when I instantly forgot just how much I had succeeded — points me back to the absurd beauty of the struggle with confidence as it relates to achievement. I got (close enough to) what I always wanted, and somebody deserving — someone I like and respect — got their own excellent news. Isn't it tragic how quickly the unaware mind can weaponize even success against itself?

Scarcity and the Comparative Mind

Who's your Ben Lerner? Who's Ben Lerner's Ben Lerner? And on the other side of the coin, whose Ben Lerner are you? I've been on both sides of the distorted equation of mental comparisons. It's interesting to discover that someone else has feelings of envy toward you. A few times someone has made themselves vulnerable enough to tell me that they envy something they believe I have. Once, a person who is creatively talented and successful in ways I could never dream of being told me he envied me. I couldn't believe it. It turns out I'm somebody's Ben Lerner, too.

We all have at least one person against whose perceived success we're measuring ourselves, and we're often the object of someone else's comparison. As shared narratives, rivalries are the stuff of legend. LeBron James, meet Michael Jordan. Jackson Pollock, meet Willem de Kooning. Rihanna, meet Beyoncé. Flintheart Glomgold, meet Scrooge McDuck.[5] Sometimes we clearly perceive what the other person has that we lack, and sometimes the mind compares vague whiffs of perception that evaporate when we try to put any language to the comparison. Sometimes we have more than one person whose success fans the winds of our inadequacies. Sometimes that little green munchkin of envy jumps from person to person like shifting targets in a shoot-'em-up video game.

We exist socially with other people, so there's an aspect of comparison that's completely natural, because it's part of our relational nature as humans. The social nature of our experience is why love and compassion are both possible, but this relational nature also causes us to gauge our own well-being by comparing ourselves to our perception of others. Our culture gives us precious few ways to define doing well that aren't comparative. What is a fulfilling career? "I have no idea," we say. "Maybe it's whatever career my most impressive friend from school is having?" What is a healthy romantic relationship? "I have no idea," we say. "Maybe it's a better relationship than my parents had?" What does it take to be a successful ally to the social and political causes you care about? "I don't know," we say. "Is it when you visibly carry more stress and rage about how fucked up things are than any *other* ally you know?" What is a successful spiritual practice? "Oh this one, this one I know! It's *enlightenment*. Amirite?" So what, then, is enlightenment? "Yeah, um...okay....I guess enlightenment is whatever I'm *not* experiencing right now."

5 Google it.

Comparative mind makes it difficult — and sometimes impossible — to acknowledge and appreciate the many successes that do come our way. And even when you aren't measuring your well-being against the perceived well-being of others, you can be devastated by a sneakier form of comparative mind: comparison to an idealized version of yourself. The problem with this comparison to Better You is that the grounds for being enough keep shifting on you. If you lose five pounds, Better You needs you to lose five more. If you get a million dollars, Better You needs two million. If you get a billion dollars, then Better You definitely needs to conquer Mars. If you get a Genius Fellowship, then next year, Better You needs you to receive a Super-Duper Genius Fellowship. With comparative mind, failures bring on all the despair in the universe, but success brings no peace. This is because comparison, by definition, leaves us no place to rest.

I often have to catch myself when I'm praising my daughter. I have a tendency to say something that sounds lovely on the face of it: "You're the best daughter ever." What I'm trying to say to her is that of all the fascinating young two-legged creatures trying to figure out how to live on planet Earth, she is the one closest to my heart. Most importantly, I'm trying to say that I'm proud of her, and that she's doing a marvelous job of being a person. But why do I have to call her the best? What message does that send? What habits of comparison does that reinforce? What pressure does it put on her to maintain her status in Dad's eyes?

Comparative mind can make us petty. We move through the world looking for reasons to disdain the success and good fortune of others. When you're locked into comparative mind, you can pass people on the street and literally get pissed at them for looking happy. *Wipe that smile off your face!* Self-reporting our pettiest thoughts can be hilarious, but it also involves much unnecessary suffering. Hence the art form known as stand-up comedy.

Economically, comparative mind has created a distorted view of what it means to possess "enough." Many people don't feel okay because they genuinely don't have enough food to eat, while a few people — who could so easily help feed those hungry folks — don't feel okay because they don't have the most gargantuan superyacht in the Mediterranean Sea.

Comparative mind is based on a mindset embedded in our dominant culture: scarcity. The political economists who created the philosophies undergirding our current system based them directly on the assumption of a scarcity of material goods. One early economic thinker was Thomas Malthus, who posited that human society would always suffer from a scarcity of resources, because even if sufficiency were temporarily attained, it would spur so much population growth that resources would become scarce once again. His vision of the world had no concept of "enoughness." He, and other early thinkers of capitalism, believed that creating barriers of scarcity was necessary to contain the rampantly discontent and eternally consumptive nature of human beings. The philosophy of scarcity is simple: human desire is unlimited, resources are finite. These thinkers framed systems of economic production that exploited human competitiveness and fear of scarcity. They saw no path for society other than constant competition and comparison.

In sports, it might be true that competition brings out humanity's highest potential. But everywhere else, this logic is iffy. In Buddhist terms, Malthus was describing human nature as a sort of "hungry ghost" realm. Recent thinkers, such as Lynne Twist, have tried to view our relationship to money and resources from a more humanistic perspective, based on a mindset of inherent abundance. But a system that promotes competition at all costs and fosters anxiety about scarcity continues to drive our resource systems over the very cliff of climate catastrophe that Malthusian logic dictates.

Uprooting this scarcity mentality requires collective and political work, as well as personal and spiritual effort. We can practice noticing comparative mind at work. When we're able to take joy in another person's success and well-being, we dissolve this sense of perceived scarcity, even if only for a moment. In this moment of sympathetic joy, we can also extract the nugget of wisdom that lies at the center of envy. The wisdom of comparative mind is that envy always shows us something we long for. When comparison becomes a fixation, it obscures our own longings by entangling our own positive desire for fulfillment with our perception of another person's experience.

When I contemplated it with a touch of humor, my Ben Lerner moment told me that I longed to return to writing fiction and poetry, when time allowed. That's it. That's all I really wanted, nothing more. When you touch in with your longing, without making it problematic to want something (because it isn't), you feel into your own sufficiency. My envy had nothing to do with Ben, except that reading his work reminds me what's possible when a writer fully tunes into their voice and craft. The person who told me he envied me simply longed for something in his own relationship to his father, it turned out. Perhaps by disclosing how he felt to me, he achieved more clarity and peace with what he wanted for himself. By understanding the longing, we realize that we don't need to compete with anyone else in order to feel like we're enough.

This experience of having and being sufficient — *enoughness* — is a state of mind that Buddhism asks us to contemplate and cultivate. In classic Buddhism the word *samsara* refers to a pervasive mentality of insufficiency, which leads to the unending — and habitually cyclical — inability to rest. There are two words in Tibetan for rejecting (or letting go of) this samsaric mind state. The first is *ngejung*, which has a quality of rising above the confusion of *samsara*. The other word is *chokshe*, which can be translated as "knowing enoughness."

Of course, Malthusian thought has dominated our human exchanges for hundreds of years. We live in a competitive world that constantly reinforces a sense of scarcity, creating anxiety not only about wealth and resources but about our social-emotional experience as well. The logic of our world dictates that without the anxiety produced by a constant fear of failure, a person won't reach their maximum productive potential. By this reasoning, if you want society to advance, you have to put a small group at the top of the heap and celebrate their achievements above all others. Otherwise, we would all lose the anxiety necessary to produce resources and move society forward.

For one sad example of this phenomenon, *MasterChef Junior* is one of the most heartwarming and entertaining television shows I've seen. A group of children ages eight through thirteen demonstrate jaw-dropping cooking skills under pressure that might make professional chefs cower. While the show is a competition, the best part is seeing how the kids develop camaraderie, supporting and rooting for each other throughout the season. At the end of the grueling competition, the winner receives $100,000 and mentorship from celebrity chefs. And what about the second-place contestant, usually another lovely child who seems almost — if not exactly — as talented as the chosen winner? Apparently a second-place finish on *MasterChef Junior* earns you precisely nothing. Sorry, kid. It's a dog-eat-dog world, or something.

The logic of scarcity is self-fulfilling. On the other hand, the logic of enoughness says that of course everyone would be motivated without the constant anxiety of scarcity, and that the persistent effects of comparative anxiety are deeply harmful to our emotional and physical health. Outside of sports, doing good work has very little to do with "beating" someone else. Anyone who has ever touched into their own enoughness knows that the joy that comes from this experience doesn't make you lazy or inert; it makes you feel joyous, rested, and revitalized. Sympathetic joy makes you want to take your seat and show up. And when you show up, whatever work you're doing starts to flow more naturally.

I often wonder how my daughter will handle the dissonant messages about success and sufficiency that will come her way as she grows up. On the one hand, her progressive education will (thankfully) send her the message that everyone is included, and everyone matters. On the other hand, only a tiny fraction of her cohort will get into their first choice of college, and by extension only a tiny percentage of them will have access to the elite institutions and perceived successes of adult life on which we still place so much value. For example, most top American universities accept students at a much lower rate than when I went to college (the acceptance rate was already pretty low, and that competitive scarcity instilled a brutal sense of anxiety in most of my classmates my senior year of high school). To create a world where successes are more easily shared, we have to dismantle the mindset that makes us consider success as an inherently scarce phenomenon. We have to replace this competitive approach with the view that accomplishment comes from developing a healthy relationship with your longing and seeing how those pursuits can create a sense of well-being that extends far beyond self-centered endeavors.

Embracing Failure, Embracing Impermanence

This chapter began with a simple story about the feeling of inadequacy that might be present in a moment of success. But what about the pain of failure, the pain of loss? Examining the pair of success and failure (sometimes translated as *gain* and *loss*) shows us how the winds of hope and fear shape the most universal experience of human life — the attempt to experience success *on our own terms*. Defining those terms is crucial in relationship to the experience of failure and loss. We constantly fail at all sorts of things we don't care about. For example, I fail to be a trained opera singer every single day of my life, but it doesn't bother me because opera has never been my thing. In order to feel we are failing at something, the mind has to identify — and care about — pursuing a goal.

Beyond meeting our basic needs — food, medicine, shelter, human connection — success and failure are constructs. It's always fun (for me, at least) to watch a sports event with someone who isn't invested at all in the rules of the game or the culture built up around the sport. The nonfan watches everyone else get hyperinvested in where the little ball goes and how everyone chases after it. The nonfan wonders aloud who these peculiar gladiators might be — examining the color palette and design of the uniforms more closely than any of the action that happens within them. The nonfan sits, confused by the what, how, and why of cheering for this or that heave of said little ball in relation to all the sculpted bodies scrambling for it like the holy grail. And what do all the hands and chests dapping and bumping each other in celebration mean? And why are those heads hung so low in defeat? *Why do you all care so much?* To the nonfan, the deeply invested fans seem like they might be on a moderate dose of hallucinogenics, or acting as gatekeepers to an alternative universe. Honestly, I feel this way whenever I'm invited to watch the Super Bowl.

I've never met a person with no longing to succeed at all. And living with these longings brings us full circle to the problematic nature of hope and expectation. The mind defines success and failure via outcomes and results. Out of a longing, we define a goal, and then the unaware mind sinks hooks into that goal as the only thing that matters. Depending on the situation, we frequently — oh so very frequently, dear reader — don't get our expectations met. And those unfulfilled expectations become known as failures. Life includes millions of these failures, and they come in all shapes and sizes. Mission not accomplished. Test not passed. Goals thwarted. Loser status, commence.

What does it feel like to fail at something you set out to do? To fail a test? To not get the job? To get fired? To have a shitty meditation session? To forget to meditate entirely? To get dumped? To lose an election? To have your creative work passed over? What does it feel like to have your body fail on you? The answer, embedded in every pairing of hope and fear we've examined so far, is the same. Failure hurts. Sometimes it hurts a little, sometimes it hurts a lot. And we need to practice acknowledging, rather than dismissing, the gorgeous ouch and heartbreak of that moment.

If you pay attention, each day includes a thousand little failures. Each meditation session is composed of one hundred little failures to inhabit the present moment. (Successful meditation has, ironically, much more to do with recognizing just a few of our failures to be present than anything else.) Each day at work is one hundred mistakes we hope no one notices. Each day of parenthood is one hundred little failures we hope neither psychologically nor physically scar our children. Each day in a relationship is one hundred failures to communicate with an open heart. Each year that passes is one hundred failed opportunities to try something we've never tried before.

The beauty of failure is the insight that comes from being present with something not working out. Holding our seats, we learn so much when we don't get what we want. Just as pain often exaggerates the sense of an immediate threat to survival, a momentary failure can exaggerate a sense of worthlessness. When you fail, your entire identity gets put on the line. But if you take the approach that there's no permanent identity to begin with, you also embrace the idea that nobody is keeping score of your successes and failures. And if nobody is keeping score, then momentary failure never signals a permanent defeat. You press the reset button and learn to run it back, as the kids like to say. Always begin again, in the words of Sharon Salzberg. Again and again, you begin again. As we train to experience impermanence, each failure becomes a growth opportunity. Loss becomes a chance not only to grieve the hopefulness that wasn't fulfilled but also to assess what wasn't working, and then to simply show up and try again.

Mindfulness of breath meditation is designed to frustrate your need to succeed. It often feels like a game with such a simple objective: *Keep your mind on the breath, damn it!* Most often, if you approach the practice like a game, you lose. You fail to stay focused on the breath. You wander. You become aware of a whole arena of thoughts, emotions, associations, song lyrics, and recipes. Over time, you may start "winning": you may develop more rapport and settledness. Eventually you might focus and concentrate more, which is a good skill in a world that suffers collectively from an attention deficit. You might even learn to enter a state of meditative equipoise, but even states of concentration are temporary. What does success at meditation get you? Do you get a sticker? And what do you notice when you "fail" at mindfulness and your mind wanders away? Success or failure, win or lose, the practice leads you to open your heart and confront your own mind. The breath is a kind of bait, which lays bare the very framework of goal orientation. The real purpose of the game is to get you to spend more time in direct relationship with yourself. Win or lose, you win the prize that really matters — the prize of awareness. You should give yourself a sticker every damn time you sit.

Success and failure are both impermanent experiences. That book I ended up writing after that "Mama, I made it!" moment now sits on my bookshelf. Am I proud of it? Sure. Was it an accomplishment? Yes. But my mind moved on from it, and I hardly think of it at all now unless someone mentions it to me. In retrospect, that moment of validation was a beautiful moment, a meaningful moment, but no more important than any other moment of success or failure I've had. I'm working on my next project, stepping into the next process, settling into the next practice session. To borrow from the Tibetan Buddhist teacher Chogyam Trungpa, the markers of our identity as humans, our accomplishments, successes, failures — these "all vanish into emptiness like the imprint of a bird in the sky."

Failure is equally transitory. Like most people, I've had some really big failures in recent years, some big experiences I've had to grieve. People died; my primary spiritual community fell apart. Of all the perceived failures and losses, the one that hit my identity the hardest was when my marriage "failed." As a child of divorce myself, I deeply wanted — and still want — to have a "successful" partnership. When the pandemic hit, it completed a process of ruptured communication and conflicting desires, as it did for so many people I know. When my wife and I split apart, I had to confront the idea that I was now a divorced child of divorce who had helped bring another child of divorce into the world.

If I was holding onto the idea that a successful marriage meant a permanent one, I would have viewed this ending as a permanent failure. Instead, my ex and I get to "begin again" as coparents and friends. Luckily, we're both able to approach our new relationship as a genuine fresh start. We consider each other very close friends. We agree that our marriage was a success, even if it was a success that ended. If there's anything I learned from the experience, it's how to relate to other people when they experience a loss or the ending of some major life situation. Instead of immediately saying "I'm so sorry to hear that" and buying into the idea that endings are automatically negative outcomes, I do my best to bite my tongue. Now, when I hear a similar story from someone else, I try to just ask "How are you?" instead.

Practicing with Comparative Mind

The main practice that Buddhism offers for working with comparative mind is called *mudita*. Often translated as "sympathetic joy," this set of contemplations involves sitting with the success or good fortune of someone you know. As you bring the person to mind, you imagine — and then share in — their embodied experience of joy or a feeling of accomplishment. Bring to mind a person you want to practice for. It's easier to start *mudita* for someone toward whom you feel no envy or rivalry, perhaps someone who has recently had success in an arena you aren't personally involved in. (For example, if you're a filmmaker, don't practice for another filmmaker. If you're trying to have a baby, don't choose a friend who just gave birth.) Bring the person's well-being or happiness to mind. You can think about some success they've had recently. Imagine opening your heart to this person. You might recite phrases and imagine saying them to the person. A few simple phrases you might try are "I'm happy for you," "May your happiness (or well-being) be sustained," and even "May this joy lead you toward awakening."

After generating joy, you can try the same practice with someone for whom you feel a bit of envy or competitive energy. If you practice for someone like that, just note the feelings that arise. Then see if you can shift ever so slightly to stay present with and share in the joy they might be feeling. This practice helps slowly unravel the scarcity mentality — the notion that another person's fulfillment comes at your expense. It may also help you gain insight into what *you* actually long for, instead of focusing on what another person might have. After working with feelings of envy for one person, you might try to extend the practice to groups of people, and eventually, to everyone, everywhere.

Contemplating the Longing to Succeed

I work with a lot of folks who want to know if it's really okay — as a Buddh-ish or mindfully inclined person — to strive for something, to want to succeed. I can only offer my opinion based on my own understanding of the path, but I believe the answer is "Hell yes!" But as you contemplate your hope for success, you might want to keep in mind the following:

- **Remember the impermanence of both success and failure.** Whether we succeed or fail, these are passing experiences being perceived from a certain vantage, a given moment in time. An individual success never guarantees any lasting well-being, and failure, too, can point to growth if we approach it as just another moment along the path. Bring to mind some success that you long for. Imagine what you will feel like the day you attain this goal. Then imagine what you will feel like a year after gaining it. A decade? And right before you die? You can then imagine failing to reach this goal, and ask yourself the same questions, using the same time frame you did for success.

- **Contemplate comparative mind.** If any aspect of your success is based on comparing yourself to or competing with someone, then notice who you're competing with. How can that comparative mentality be transformed into a deeper understanding of your own longing? Can the person you're comparing yourself to be transformed into an inspiration? Is there any way you can understand your longing to succeed without making comparisons? Is that possible? If it doesn't feel possible, put a pin in this question and continue to contemplate it in the future.
- **Contemplate enoughness.** If I achieve success in what I long to do, how will I experience contentment, or enoughness? What does enoughness feel like for me? When have I felt it before? What bodily sensations, thoughts, or emotions do I associate with it? How can I make the experience of enoughness more sustainable, not just when I achieve my goals, but as I proceed on my journey?

The Four Powers of Confidence

We've talked in depth about eight forces that can knock us off our seats and make us feel fragile. In the second section of this book, we explore four powerful aids for increasing our capacity to connect with inherent confidence: compassion, lineage, awareness, and windhorse. By working with these powerful allies, we start tapping into something much deeper and more omnipresent than a set of "hacks" for working with hope and fear. This is — dare I say it — a sort of unconditional confidence that any of us can access. When we tap into the aspects of the confidence that exists innately in all humans, we can start to hold our seats more fully, whichever way the wind blows.

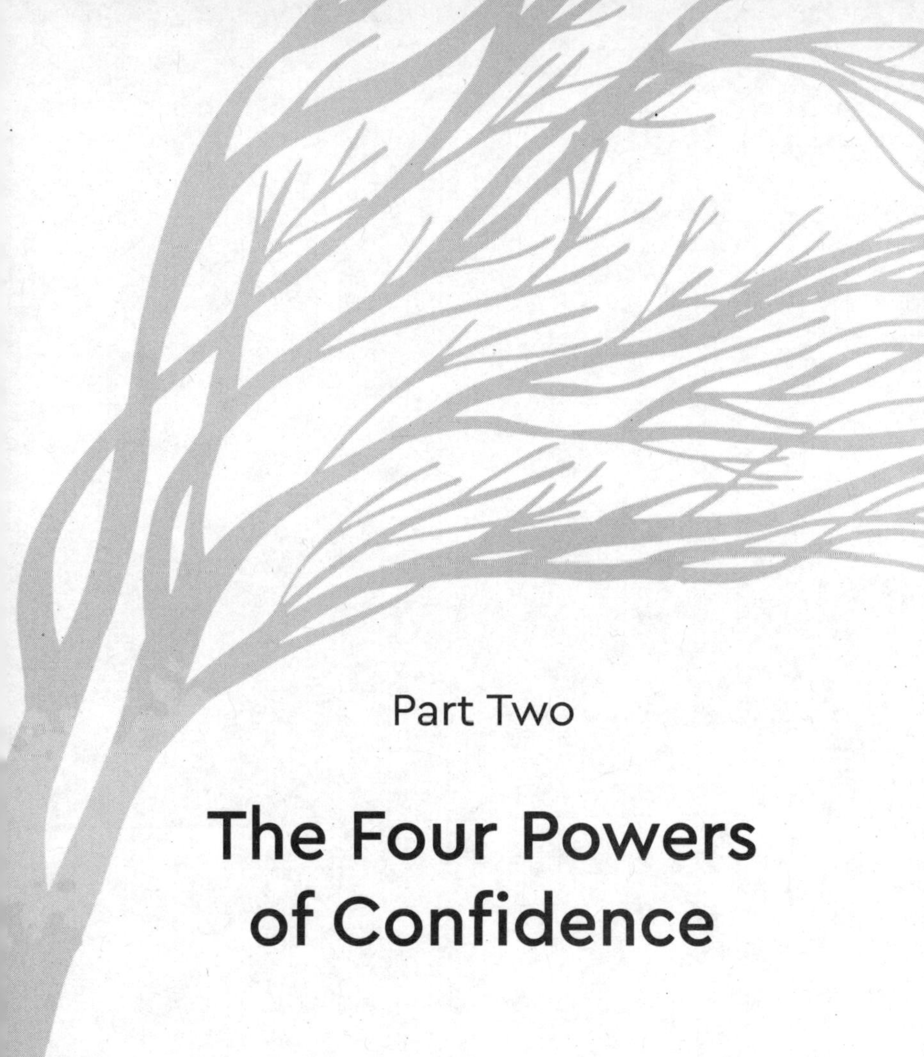

Part Two

The Four Powers of Confidence

CHAPTER SIX

The Power of Compassion

No one who has ever touched liberation could possibly want anything other than liberation for everyone.

— Reverend angel Kyodo williams

I'm not a "sports" guy, but I do love to watch basketball. My favorite player, since the beginning of his career, has been Kevin Durant (widely known as KD). In 2014, KD won the NBA's Most Valuable Player award, effectively naming him the best on the planet for that year. I watched his acceptance speech live. For an athlete accepting an award, the speech is really long — twenty-six minutes long, to be exact. If this were the Academy Awards, the music would have started and they would have cut to a commercial before KD even got warmed up.

The first 90 percent of the speech is sweet, conveying a tender form of masculinity that our world could use much more of. But as it goes on, KD's speech borders on tedium. He takes extra time to directly acknowledge every last one of his teammates and team staff, as well as everyone else involved in his professional success. I appreciated his care and thoroughness, but at a few moments, the minute details of his gratitude provoked irritation. *Come on, KD! We get it! You don't need to thank the third-string point guard for a full minute!* Still, KD's attention to the shared nature of his success as a team athlete shines through. For acknowledging an individual award, his words are full of the pronouns *you* and *we*, and short on the pronoun *I*.[1]

After twenty-four minutes of thanking pretty much every single human he's ever worked with, KD turns to his mother, Wanda, who single-parented Kevin and his three siblings in the unnecessarily cruel struggle that is American poverty. KD grows more emotional and says to his mom: "I don't think you know what you did." He and his mother both start crying as he turns back to the assembled guests: "When something good happens to you…I don't know about you guys, but I tend to look back at what got me here." It's unique to hear a professional athlete describe being the best in the world as something that "happened to him," rather than something he accomplished. KD goes on to talk about how Wanda carried their family through their many struggles. Still addressing his mother as both are weeping harder, he closes his speech with "You're the real MVP."

If we want anything good to happen, we have to realize what KD realized in his speech — our own good fortune depends on other people. Nobody accomplishes anything on their own, ever. Practicing compassion opens our eyes to the

---

1 A friend who works in fashion and advertising once produced a photo shoot with KD and reported the same. Unlike the vast majority of celebrities she had worked with, KD took time to carefully acknowledge every single person on the set.

interconnections between us and helps us remember that we're part of a much larger network of beings, all trying to achieve their own well-being and fulfill their deepest aspirations. Seeing our labor as interwoven with the efforts of others gives the needed context to a personal path. Compassion helps overcome our deep-seated tendency toward individualism, a worldview that makes our experience increasingly small, isolated, fearful, and aggressive.

Practicing compassion is the first support for working with confidence. Why? Compassion allows us to see our struggles, our actions, and our lives in a larger context. In those moments where we're striving to achieve some purpose or outcome for ourselves, we tend to develop tunnel vision. We might grow increasingly myopic and self-involved. The drive for success can obscure the experiences of those around us. When I'm nervous about showing up for something important, it becomes harder to maintain perspective and consider the experience of others. When we get myopic, we also get claustrophobic and reactive, and that's when it's harder to hold our seat.

Of course, the world is full of remarkable individuals, and we need to honor their power and achievements. The MVP is a personal award. It was invented because even though basketball is a team sport, people felt a need to acknowledge one player's strength, skill, and effort. But never — not once in the whole history of humanity — has a single person manifested their power all by themselves. The mythos of individualism — the idea that success is entirely self-generated — has woven itself so deeply into our cultural narratives that it has become almost invisible, the air we breathe. The individualist narrative has only two components: what obstacles I faced and how I overcame them. It decontextualizes and oversimplifies success, reducing it to a series of personal trials, tribulations, and conquests. Narratives of this kind almost always diminish the role of environmental supports and privilege. Successful people who argue that they "manifested" their goals solely through their own efforts always exhibit a subtle defensiveness, a fear that observers will look behind the curtain. Someone who defensively claims to be a "self-made" billionaire doesn't want you to know they started out with a trust fund and family contacts who gave them plenty of help, time and time again.

The individualistic worldview relies on the pretense that one person has conquered all obstacles through Herculean efforts. But even Herculean courage is a trait we learn from those who surround us, and especially those who came before in our lineages. People are often surprised to learn that the Buddha did not teach himself to meditate. He grew up privileged and highly educated, and when he left his home, he studied with two learned meditation teachers, whose work he took further, reinterpreted, and expanded upon. Elon Musk — currently the richest man in the world and one of the loudest proclaimers of the philosophy of individualism alive — would have very little without his inherited fortune, or without the achievements of his company's namesake — Nikola Tesla — and countless other scientists and entrepreneurs who came before. That's not to say Elon did nothing. He's clearly helped create quite a lot of technical innovations. But no one is self-made. The more emphatically a person attributes all their success to individual effort, the more unacknowledged support and extracted labor usually lies right behind their facade.

Modern writers who focus on systems of patriarchy and

white supremacy position individualism as a direct product of those centuries-old systems.[2] Buddhist philosophy doesn't locate individualism in any specific cultural system, but instead frames it as a general worldview that might exist in any cultural context, a worldview built on mistaken ideas of causality — that is, confusion about how events happen. The basic metaphysics of individualism goes like this: the cause of an outcome (like being the best basketball player on Earth, becoming a successful artist, or becoming "enlightened") is entirely self-generated. The individual alone makes their success through some secret recipe that's one part hard work and one part superhuman intelligence or skill, and zero parts anything they got from (or owe back to) anyone else. If a person becomes ten thousand times richer than anyone else, it's because they're ten thousand times smarter and work ten thousand times harder (which is both physically and mentally impossible, not to mention insulting). If the individualist wins a championship, their success is entirely due to their own effort and abilities. The "self" accomplishes it all and therefore owns the credit for all those personal accomplishments.

And on the flip side, individualism contains an even crueler philosophy of blame. If you haven't succeeded — if you haven't "manifested" your potential — you alone are to blame.

---

2 My dear friend and badass dharma teacher Kate Johnson — author of the book *Radical Friendship* — introduced me to the work of Kenneth Jones and Tema Okun. In their manual *Dismantling Racism: A Workbook for Social Change Groups*, they describe individualism as one of the ten main attributes of white supremacy culture. Patriarchy's myth of the heroic male savior acting alone is so deeply entrenched that it's difficult to find a history of any region or period that doesn't highlight it.

You haven't figured out the winning personal formula (enter an entire field of "self-help" books), or you haven't worked hard enough, or you simply don't have what it takes. Tough luck, kid. Maybe next lifetime.

We know that the truth is much more complex. Individuals do make things happen, but they do it in a supportive context. We need a worldview that places individual effort in the framework of interdependence. Practicing compassion provides us with that framework and leads to a differently embodied experience of connection.

Equalizing Self and Other

You may be sick of talking about compassion. Many of us suffer from some level of compassion fatigue, so discussing the power of compassion related to building our confidence can be deflating, rather than inspiring. You might be having this response: "I already do so much thinking about others, and it's overwhelming. I'm *exhausted.* I want to talk about my own needs and settle into my own power for a change. How do I do that?" A lot of compassion fatigue is induced by technology. We know far more about suffering in the modern world than ever before. In earlier times, we wouldn't be able to immediately know about a mass shooting one hundred miles away, the outbreak of a new virus a thousand miles away, or the outbreak of a war ten thousand miles away. Our hearts are called daily to stretch like taffy, to feel an overwhelming level of empathy as we receive the news of any given day on planet Earth. These events can hurt our hearts so much they feel like they're constantly breaking. Unless we want the sheer scope of human suffering to overwhelm us, we have to find some way to increase our hearts' capacity.

We often operate on a highly moralistic — and therefore exhausting — idea of compassion, which makes us feel forever deficient in our quest to care about the world. Compassion is usually framed as putting others before yourself. While — in moments of greed or self-obsession — this aspect of compassion is sometimes what we need to hear, we have to understand compassion more globally. If we look at compassion only as helping others, then we end up feeling that any moment spent contemplating our own needs is intrinsically selfish. In this mindset, self-care is perceived as a moral failure. But we're all human, with human needs, and we can't think only about others all the time if we want to survive or thrive. The problem with moral imperatives ("I *should* be more compassionate") is that they bring with them a feeling of judgment — both judging others and judging ourselves. If you place yourself under a moral imperative to think of others as something you're just *supposed to* do, you'll also come to regard yourself as a spiritual failure, as a bad person. There's no joy in this approach to compassion, because you're forever feeling inadequate to the task. That which is joyless is also exhausting. Feeling this joyless deficiency is the root of compassion fatigue. If you take the approach that compassion is a moral obligation, something you are required to perform all the time, you will forever feel subtle guilt and shame over taking up space yourself.

The archetype for compassion in Buddhism is the bodhisattva, the being who sees their own awakening as undeniably and inextricably tied to the well-being of others. Rather than viewing compassion as a moral imperative, the bodhisattva relates to it as a perceptual experience, a *feeling* of connection. This is a key difference. Compassion is not a directive, it's an *experience*. Compassion meditation asks us to try to open our hearts to others, but first and foremost it asks us — very explicitly — to open our hearts to *ourselves*. Even ancient treatises on *tonglen* compassion meditation instruct students to always begin the process by directing compassion inward, toward our own struggles and needs. In contemporary language, this is called self-compassion. Only after practicing self-compassion do we move on to directing compassion toward those around us. Eventually, compassion practice asks us to open our hearts to both self and others at the same time, to see if we can touch the true interconnectedness that exists without boundaries, beyond the myth of individualism. This is called "equalizing self and other."

Why is equalizing self and other — rather than martyrdom — considered the most mature articulation of compassion? It's not because of any moralizing involved in the experience. Rather, it's because of the felt experience of those instances of open-heartedness that we each glimpse all the time. These are the moments when the concepts of self and other — all those irrelevant questions of who "deserves" love the most — momentarily fall away. When we can tap into this experience of interconnectedness, the feeling of care starts to move naturally wherever it needs to go, without being held back by any conceptual framework of who "deserves" compassion. If care needs to be pointed inward toward your own well-being, it goes there without any second-guessing. You receive the love you need. If you need a good night's sleep, you do what it takes to get one. If you need cheese, you eat the damn cheese. Simple as that. If care needs to go toward other beings, then your heart moves in that direction, and you help them however you are able. When self and other are equalized, everyone is included in the scope of care, and all those countless *should*s evaporate for just a moment. You can imagine equalizing self and other in Oprah Winfrey's voice of abundance: "I get some love! And you get some love! And you get some love! And we get some love! *Everybody* gets some love!"

This is why the quote at the beginning of this chapter from Reverend angel Kyodo williams is so powerful. She frames collective liberation as a direct experience rather than a moral imperative. Anybody who has touched the felt experience of life beyond fixed concepts of self and other would long for the same experience for all other beings as well. In the moments of feeling most open, you have indeed had this experience, even if it's only a fleeting one, so far.

The Three Aspects of Compassion

In the classic Buddhist tradition, teachings on compassion are framed and arranged in multiple ways. As the result of practicing these teachings on compassion, as well as learning from modern Western psychology,[3] I've come to see compassion

3 The work of Kristin Neff, Christopher Germer, and Kelly McGonigal has been key in understanding the psychological and scientific function of compassion. A lecture by McGonigal that I had the honor of facilitating was especially formative in crystallizing my own articulation of these three core aspects of compassion, which are different from Neff's three components of self-compassion. My understanding comes from examining the mechanics of *tonglen* meditation, the teachings of how a bodhisattva engages in the world, and the work of various other modern teachers.

as having three basic elements: empathy, care (sympathy), and agency (taking action). These three components are the same whether you are directing compassion toward yourself, toward others, or inward and outward at the same time.

Empathy

Empathy is the ground floor of compassion. Simply put, it's the ability to imagine what someone else is feeling *from their own side*. Empathy is a crucial social skill for living in a complex and interdependent world. When we practice compassion meditation for somebody, we start simply by imagining the experience of that person. All we do at first is try to tap into their experience in any way we can. Empathy takes attention and mindfulness. We have to be able to hold a person in awareness long enough to grow curious about their experience, to slow down and ask, "So who is this person and what might they be experiencing?"

When you practice self-compassion, you're taking time to reflect on your own experience rather than just trudging through life like a drone without an operator. Instead of waking up in the morning and saying "Shit, I have seventeen things I need to do before lunch," you take a moment to reflect on what it *feels* like to have seventeen things to do. Self-empathy can be like a little private conversation with yourself.

I ask, What does it feel like to be Ethan with seventeen things to do?

Well, Ethan, it feels pretty stressful, actually. It makes me wish I were a superintelligent, hyperagile octopus. And that makes me feel a little inadequate for only being a moderately intelligent, slightly clumsy two-armed creature. I also feel a little resentful of the seventeen things and everybody who asked me to do them. And it makes me especially resentful of the things on the list that nobody even asked me to do! Why did I do this to myself again?

I hear you, Ethan, I say back. So you feel stressed, inadequate, and a little resentful. Did I get that right?

Yup, Ethan, I say. You got it.

That moment we reflect on the *quality* of our own experience — rather than just being mired in the details of life — is a moment of self-empathy. It's the first part of inward-facing (or self-) compassion. Likewise, the first step of compassion toward others is a willingness to ask yourself the imaginative question, What's it like to be them? The single word *imagine* is the key to avoid projecting our own experience onto others. Because we can't know for sure how someone else is feeling, we need to be humble about our outward-facing empathy. Because it is based on perception, empathy can be speculative, projective, and sometimes embarrassingly inaccurate regarding another person's embodied experience. It takes a lot of patience and mindfulness to even empathize with yourself, to understand your own feelings in a given moment. Never mind others — sometimes knowing what you alone are feeling requires the ongoing guidance of another person.

Some of us are quite empathic. But those of us who identify as empaths can also make mistakes when reporting on another person's experience. Sometimes when I'm working with a student and I really pay attention, I feel like I *get them*, like I know what's happening inside them. Parents also want to feel like we "get" our kids. But we need to realize that empathy is always an approximation, at best. Not only is it impossible to know with certainty what another being is experiencing, but, like ours, their experience is constantly in flux. Even if we pin it down in a given moment, that experience will not last. Empathy is a process that requires constant verification. We need to ask the person we're empathizing with, "Did I get that right?" And we need to ask that question regardless of how well we think we know them.

My daughter and I pass a number of crossing guards on our way to and from her school. There's one crossing guard we've gotten to know pretty well. I'm embarrassed to say we built up a fond rapport with her, full of cheerful banter, for at least a month before I remembered to ask her name. Such is the reflexive anonymity of life in a metropolis. Her name is Tina. Now, Tina has a certain Jekyll and Hyde demeanor. Toward bipedal beings in the neighborhood — pedestrians, parents, children — she's a sweet auntie who cares for you, asks after you when she hasn't seen you in a minute, and keeps you safe. But toward that wheel-going community — truck drivers, motorcyclists, and all those cars with New Jersey license plates who are needlessly aggressive about making that left turn — whew boy! Tina is all out of effs to give, barking admonishments and shaking her head. To them, she's a frustrating human speed bump. Because of empathy, she's no longer an abstraction to me. She's Tina.[4]

How many people have just been extras on the set of your

4 On the last day of school, when she was retiring from her job as crossing guard, Tina handed out small presents to all the kids she had protected throughout the year. She even came all the way into the neighborhood park and playground to find all the children she knew to whom she hadn't given presents yet.

daily life? From the vantage of a life lived without empathy, humans become cold objects and fleshy abstractions. A school crossing guard is an annoyance slowing down your commute, a faceless public entity useful only as a means to keep your child safe, or a person whose triumphs and hardships are of no importance to you at all. *Who even cares about the inner experience of a school crossing guard? That doesn't have anything to do with me. I got enough problems.*

And still a moment comes, a moment when a Tina-like being flashes across the GPS of your awareness, and something calls you to ask: *So what's it like to be a school crossing guard?* You feel your way into that question and see what information comes back. And then you feel deeper. *So what's Tina's story? What does it feel like to be Tina right now? What is the nature of Tina-ness?* Sometimes you get to ask the person these questions. But on the meditation seat, you have only your memory and your imagination. The imaginative curiosity that it takes to ask those questions, along with the responses that come back to you when you inquire — that's empathy.

Empathy is the first step, but empathy alone is not compassion. If you wanted to, you could imagine, investigate, and research the nature of a person's experience in order to manipulate them, abuse them, or profit from their behaviors. I could watch Tina all day because I want to cut budgets and figure out how artificial intelligence might replace her. Or I could just try to charm Tina, scheming for special treatment when I'm driving by, so I can get to work faster and beat my competitors in my quest for world domination. Empathy alone is a neutral skill. But once we invest in it, empathy has a tendency to open our hearts. Without inquiring into the experience of others, any care or concern we try to develop for them will be distanced, vague, and imprecise. Without empathy, at best, when we care about others, we're pitying them. At worst, we may cause harm as we're trying to help, because we have no idea who we're dealing with.

Care

The second aspect of compassion is sympathy, or care. Care goes beyond imagining another person's experience to developing genuine concern for their well-being and wishing them happiness *from their own perspective.* "I hope they don't suffer. I hope they have what they need. I hope they stay safe. I hope they're happy, whatever that means to them." There are all sorts of potential obstacles here that classic Buddhism identifies. First, care is often offered conditionally, based on the fulfillment of perfectionist expectations. "I hope I'm happy…unless I make a mistake. Because if I screw up, like yesterday, then I will deserve to feel miserable." Or how about "I'll love you until the day I die (or until the moment you disappoint me)"?

Care is both a blessing and a burden. Care resensitizes you, and it can weigh on you like a stone. It's a bit inconvenient to care about crossing guards, to find yourself researching whether or not they have good salaries or healthcare plans. Likewise, becoming a parent, you start to feel a little differently about every child you see, almost like you need to make sure they're *all* okay and not about to hurt themselves. I also have a growing person in front of me each day who looks quite a lot like I did as a child. In becoming a parent, I grew more tender toward my own inner kid. It's a bit inconvenient to find yourself tearing up in public for no particular reason. In experiencing care, we start to notice a contrast with the ways we've grown numb and frozen toward ourselves and others.

We also start to notice why going numb makes so much sense: it feels safer and much less of a burden. Sometimes it feels more compassionate to stay numb, especially when we're powerless to help in any meaningful way. Tourists in some cities are instructed to ignore unhoused or poor people begging for help, on the premise that interacting with them or giving them money will only cause more trouble for everyone involved. Many professions run on similar norms of desensitization, just to get the job done with limited emotional resources in the face of abundant suffering. Going numb is not a deficiency, it's a self-preservation response. In trying to build my own capacity for compassion, I've developed more understanding of why I might seek to shut people and situations out of my consciousness. There's a real intelligence behind that numbness, and I've learned to generate compassion for that intelligence as well. There's a good reason we often move through the world with our heads down. There's a good reason we sometimes say, "I just can't right now."

When you care, you're letting in feelings and emotions rather than shielding yourself against their presence. Sometimes we just don't feel up to experiencing that level of sensitivity toward humanity. And even when we do feel up to the task, there are an awful lot of other beings here to care about.[5] Many of those beings don't seem to be doing particularly well, even those with

5 The mathematician and animal rights activist Brian Tomasik estimates that there are about twenty quintillion (or twenty billion billion) beings on Earth. Just imagine the number of sentient beings who might exist in this galaxy!

lots of privilege. Practicing compassion is like training a muscle, and our muscles get tired as they train. As with any other form of exercise, sometimes you have to take a break.

This can also mean taking a break from difficult relationships. All the recent discourse in various wellness, psychology, and activist communities about setting boundaries suggests that this is an aspect of compassion that most of us have never learned. We have to understand that setting boundaries is done in the service of compassion, not in the service of avoiding discomfort. Sure, I could decide I was going to ignore every school crossing guard I passed and convince myself I was just "setting a boundary." I could ghost all the people in my life and call that setting boundaries. But this wouldn't necessarily be setting boundaries with well-being in mind. It'd actually just be acting like a jerk.

I greatly appreciate the word *titrate*. In the context of medical care, *titration* refers to the need to introduce a medicine according to the tolerance and needs of the body. When it comes to the caring piece of compassion, we need to titrate our experience of the world's suffering. This requires some amount of self-care, along with some amount of boundary-setting. It almost always requires putting some distance between ourselves and certain difficult or unhealthy relationships. But when we set boundaries, we need to be clear about our intention. From a Buddhist standpoint, it's not possible to shut out sentient beings permanently. We're all too connected. When dealing with difficult, draining, or harmful relationships, I've learned to ask, Do I want this relationship to be an active relationship right now? Is this a relationship that is helpful to cultivate at this moment, or do I need to take a step back?

I have had to ask myself this question many times because my early style was to be accommodating and take on too much, in both personal relationships and work situations. It would often (read: almost always) lead to subtle resentment of personal relationships and a feeling of being overworked in my livelihood. I constantly felt like I was negotiating against myself. Over time, through a variety of subtle and not-so-subtle smacks in the face, I learned how to create work relationships in which parties feel clear and good about what's expected of us. More slowly, I've learned to increasingly participate in personal relationships that are mutually fulfilling, with good communication about expectations, and with the possibility of repairing harm when one of us hurts the other, or when both people hurt each other.

Sometimes I counsel students on setting boundaries in their familial relationships, which can bring up all kinds of intense feelings and primal fears. The fears of saying no to your family grow louder if we're trying to study Buddhism and adopt its compassionate worldview. Nothing can undercut confidence and make you worry you might be selfish more than deciding not to be in active relationship with a member of your own family. Making the decision to step away is always hard, but we need to learn the limits to how much we can keep in awareness and active relationship at any one time.

The great thing about formal compassion meditation is that it doesn't require an active relationship with the person for whom you practice. You can decide that you can't deal with a person — that you have to take a break — and still include them in your practice. A person doesn't have to be present in your life to be present in your practice.

At the end of the day, the good — and bad — news is that you can't cut anyone off permanently. We are all interdependent. My exhale eventually becomes the inhale of the person with whom I disagree the most politically, and your exhale becomes the inhale of the ex with whom you had your unhealthiest relationship. And for that reason, whenever we can open the gates a little more and let more into our awareness — even if not into our active relationships — we practice staying in relationship to all beings. And we find ourselves feeling both more sensitive and more alive. That's the timeless benefit of caring.

Agency

The third part of compassion is the power of action, or agency. The third quality is the revolutionary part of the equation. With action, we see the truth of something Dr. King said so well: "Power without love is reckless and abusive, and love without power is sentimental and anemic." Without agency, compassion can feel like *A Clockwork Orange*, as if someone handcuffed us to a seat in a private movie theater, propped our eyes open, and forced us to watch an endless stream of horrors. We are often taught to view compassion as the relinquishing of our power rather than the expression of it. Within the worldview of individualism, compassion has come to be treated as something that is morally praiseworthy and great for a person's PR, but also draining, weakening, and inconvenient. Compassion — it seems — takes something away from the person who practices it, rather than giving them something. An act of compassion is something for which you get good karma points (Narrator: That's not a thing) rather than a mutually empowering action.

But true compassion is empowering and replenishing to the person who practices it. True compassion is uplifting. True compassion is relieving. True compassion has *agency*.

In the *tonglen* compassion meditation, you imagine a being who is suffering or confused, and you breathe in that suffering or confusion. That sounds a little overwhelming, but you don't get stuck with the suffering, because that's only the first part of the process, the part of the practice related to empathizing. As you breathe in, you imagine that your body is not solid, almost holographic, and that as you stay present, the energy of suffering is transformed into wisdom and healing. By imagining this transformation within your breathing cycle, you rewire yourself to believe in your own capacity to work with difficult experience, rather than being overwhelmed as you take it into your system. Then, having imagined your body transforming the confusion, you breathe that healing light or breath out toward the suffering being. As you breathe out, you imagine yourself sending something helpful to the person for whom you are practicing. You imagine the outbreath having a positive impact, even if it's only microscopic.

What you send out to the person in need isn't as important as your intention as you exhale. You could breathe out light or pure air, or a phrase like "May you be free of suffering." You can imagine sending something simple and useful that might reduce their turmoil. If the person is tired, you can imagine sending them the comfiest pillow on Earth as you exhale. The power of compassion meditation begins with its inherent agency and creativity. As you exhale something positive, you remind yourself that suffering is neither permanent nor necessary. You can always work with the situation, even if you can't solve it completely. As you rise from the practice, you think, "Maybe I can do something about this." As the classic Buddhist teachings note, we don't just aspire to create an awakened heart, we also act to make it so.

In the months and weeks before the 2022 midterm elections, most of the conversations I had with friends and students included an ominous discussion of election anxiety. Trumpism had lost in 2020 because of a ton of collective hard work and effort. But now, two years later, a flood of private election polls made it seem like the midterms were going to be a wipeout, just as the 2010 and 2014 midterms had been. It seemed like the road was being reset for Trump's party to take the presidency in 2024, and American democracy to fall soon afterward.

"Are you afraid?" I was asked constantly.

"Yup, of course," I'd answer.

"How do you deal with your anxiety when you look at all these polls in the news?"

I'd reply, "I'm not watching the polls very much because they're unreliable, other than maybe to tell the campaign where to focus effort. I'm writing letters to voters in swing districts in North Carolina via the Vote Forward platform. I'm going to go down to North Carolina the weekend before the election to volunteer and knock on doors. Every time I freak out, I write another letter. I imagine the individual person that I'm writing to, and what it might feel like if they go vote. It's helping me feel a lot more grounded. You could try it."

I've never gotten over the fear of knocking on a stranger's door and reminding them to vote. But I can't tell you how much these actions helped me in the fall of 2022. They helped me turn fear into tiny little moments of action. They turned the situation from a horror movie I was being forced to watch on social media into a workably messy reality in which I could participate. They helped me get out of my head and connect. If you ever suffer from political anxieties like these, I highly recommend direct volunteering as a form of compassion practice. It didn't even matter that with one exception, every local NC race and the senatorial race for which I volunteered and wrote letters ended with just about the same 51–49 percent loss. I had found my outbreath. I had used my agency. I felt connected and basically good. I made new friends through volunteering. The action was the compassion, and it benefited both myself and others. The results were mixed, but we can always begin again. There's always another practice session — and another election — coming.

People often forget about breathing out in compassion meditation. Breathing out is the agency piece. It's the moment where you remind yourself that although you may not be able to cure confusion or harm, you might be able to do something simple to help. Breathing out is soothing, and not because of some magic that heals suffering. The outbreath rewires us to remember the mutual benefit of doing something impactful. Don't ever breathe in without breathing out. Don't practice taking in the pain of the world without also contemplating your own agency. If you only breathe in suffering, it makes sense that you won't feel so great about your practice — or your respiratory system.

Without taking action, we're left with the vacuity of the "thoughts and prayers" model of compassion. When yet another mass shooting occurs in the United States, and a certain

US senator from Texas (to name a personal favorite of mine among the many who've repeatedly voted against sensible assault-weapon restrictions) offers "thoughts and prayers" to the victims and their families, why does his statement anger us so rightfully? It's because this senator has real agency to stop something bad from happening, and he's pretending that he doesn't. He's hoping the media conveys only his caring quote and not his lack of action. The wise part of us knows that something is way off here, or at least incomplete. This expression of compassion isn't only anemic, it's cynical. This man could very easily change his vote and thereby express the agency of his prayers as well. The stench of his cynicism overpowers any genuine wishes that his prayers might contain.

Back to Tina, our beloved crossing guard. On a simple interpersonal level, active compassion might mean asking Tina if she wanted me to bring her a cup of coffee when I passed a deli on a cold and rainy day. (She always kindly refused this gesture, by the way. It seems the idea of receiving help from another person made her a little nervous, a hesitation to which I can also relate.) And whenever we take a simple action to ease our own turmoil or stress, we are likewise experiencing the power of self-compassion.

Still, it's important that compassion extend beyond the personal or the interpersonal level to the systemic or collective level. Just as my compassion practice might lead me to ask if Tina herself needs anything, compassion can also make me want to research the broader conditions in which she works. Interpersonal compassion means giving Tina a smile or a cup of coffee. Systemic compassion means calling my city councilperson to advocate for an increase in the health benefits of crossing guards. To act compassionately, we need to both care for individuals and advocate for good within our social and political systems. Otherwise, compassion meditation becomes nothing but a more psychologically rigorous form of "thoughts and prayers."

CHAPTER SEVEN

The Power of Lineage

Long ago, the story goes, three spiritual seekers wandered separately through the wilderness looking for a teacher. By coincidence, their paths converged. They had each come a great distance, steeped in the exhaustion of journeys filled with obstacles and mishaps. Realizing they were headed to the same town, they decided to share supplies for the remaining distance. As they neared the settlement, feeling the anticipation of arrival, their conversation went from muted to increasingly cheerful. They asked each other why they had come to this place, seeking out a new teacher. The three travelers quickly realized they were looking for the same person.

Each of them had heard that this teacher was a great master. Each traveler had teachers before, but for each, something had been left incomplete. Their former teachers had — in different ways — left them frustrated, churning in dissatisfaction and self-doubt. Sometimes the teachers' insights had disappointed. Sometimes the students witnessed reactions toward other students that made them doubt the teacher's patience and generosity. One teacher, the third traveler said, had even become physically abusive, slapping and hitting students.

Something had been rekindled in each of the three when they heard the name of this new teacher. Just as when they'd first begun their studies, each felt the renewed urge to know reality, the wish to embrace truth, and above all the curiosity they had felt when they were new on the path. This was the passion they remembered feeling when everything had been fresh, before the scars of frustration had left them cynical and defeated.

This teacher, they had heard, could take you directly to awakening in ways that few, if any, other teachers in this world could match. This master did not stumble over words, did not get caught up in overcomplications of logic. This teacher's presence radiated for miles with a healing smile, words and actions aligning like a flawless piece of machinery. This teacher, they heard, was a master.

When they reached the town, they asked the teacher's whereabouts in the local tavern. They were pointed to a place on the outskirts of town where the master dwelled alone and received students each morning for interviews and requests.

The three students saw the sun setting in the sky and found a place to sleep for the night, impatient to have to wait out another sunrise. The next morning, they knocked at the door of the teacher's modest cottage as early as they could without seeming impolite. The master hugged each of them warmly, offered them tea, and asked them a few questions about their lives.

"I can see none of you is new to this path," the teacher said. "While you have traveled far on foot, none of you arrives here with innocence. You all have minds full of ideas. The fresh longing that would make your awakening easy, like the natural blooming of a flower in its season, is absent in each of you."

The master continued: "That childlike wonder is required for a worthy vessel to receive this wisdom. You each bring the heavy baggage of your old notions, tired frames of reference, half-forgotten notes, lessons learned from other sources. Unfortunately, much of what you have acquired has served only to deepen your subtle habits, not liberate you from them. I can see this sad truth in the lines on each of your faces. So we must start afresh together. I must ask you to renounce all your former teachers and everything you may have learned from them. You must present yourself here like a clean cup to receive the tea I serve, fresh and hot. You must offer yourself to this work as a blank canvas on which the truth can be rendered. That can only start when your past confusion is erased and forgotten."

The first student began to interrupt the master eagerly, like a puppy panting, but the master waved them off.

"I don't want you to answer right now. I know this is much to ask, and it is never wise to make such proclamations hastily. Go and sleep in the hamlet and come back tomorrow morning with your answers." The first traveler seemed disappointed to have to wait even longer to begin their studies. The second wore a blank expression, not sure exactly what to think or say. The third left the cottage wearing a deep frown, discomfited by the exchange.

They returned to the humble abode the next morning. The master did not even rise to greet them today, much less offer hugs, but waved them to be seated on the cushions around the room. They felt the master observing them with a penetrating gaze.

"Have you considered my conditions for guiding you?" the teacher asked.

All three nodded.

"What are your answers, then?"

The first jumped in almost before the question was finished. "My last teacher was a phony, a charlatan, and on top of that, a complete and utter idiot." The traveler's hands moved wildly. "I learned nothing. I denounce my last teacher completely. I wish I'd never met that loser! What a waste of everyone's time! Dearest master, beacon of light in the darkness of *samsara*, I await the splendor of your unparalleled teachings. I wish I had been able to bask in your glory much sooner!" The first student bowed and prostrated deeply.

The master's expression did not change while turning to the second student, who shifted forward.

This student was less verbose. "I agree to what you asked," the student said, voice shaking slightly. "I denounce my previous teachers and all I have learned." The second student, seemingly unsure of what to do, slowly mimicked the first and prostrated as well.

The teacher pointed at the third student, whose face looked pained.

"I'm sorry," the third student said, looking at the other two travelers. "Like both of you, I traveled a long and arduous path to reach this place. My old teacher, I now believe, was not fully trustworthy. He asked me to give up all facades, yet he remained hidden. He said many things I disagreed with and left little room for my own experience. I have heard stories of him cheating students out of their money, abusing some, and various other rumors of wrongdoing. And yet there was wisdom in what he offered, and I made progress along my practice when I followed his instructions. I touched aspects of the truth when

I studied with him. And those experiences are part of what has led me here. Even if some of his lessons taught me what *not* to do, those lessons also were of value. I am here now both because of what I learned before and because it was necessary to move on. I cannot deny any of these facts any more than I can deny that I'm here with you now.

"I come to you to learn how to trust myself and gain freedom from confused beliefs," the third student continued, "but I find, ironically, that I must already trust myself before I start. Maybe that's the real lesson in what you asked. Or maybe you're just as controlling as my last teacher was. I realize that you want us to be like a blank canvas. I understand how previous stains might corrupt a fresh beginning. But I think a clean beginning is neither possible nor desirable for me. Perhaps I'm forgoing a huge opportunity in saying no to your request. But in my heart, this doesn't feel right at all. Thank you for your time." The third student bowed respectfully to the master and turned to leave the cottage, preparing for the long and uncertain journey back home.

"Wait," the teacher called, suddenly softening in demeanor. "Please wait." The teacher turned to the other two students, who were growing unsettled, a sinking suspicion creeping into the room as the master's body shifted.

The teacher pointed at the first student, the one who had wholeheartedly denounced their previous learning. "Do you think I'm a fool?" The teacher's voice suddenly filled the room and shook the cottage walls. "Answer me this: Why would *any* teacher take you on as a student? You will just denounce me too, someday, and probably you'll do so easily, as soon as I disappoint the self-serving admiration that you now signal so fondly. You tell me what I want to hear just to get what you want from me. What a transactional approach! Devotion is simply respect and gratitude, not these saccharine gestures you insist on making. Your fake worship will ferment into resentment. I see how this ends, and personally, I want none of your charade. If you can't respect the journey that brought you here, how will you ever respect our journey together, or any of the journeys that lie ahead for you? Get out of here!" The first student started to protest but soon discovered the futility of doing so. The student left, and the second student started to follow. The master stopped the second student. "Please consider my words carefully, and come back tomorrow. If you would like to do so, you'd be welcome to join us." The second student nodded slowly and left.

After the two had departed, a smile crossed the master's face. The room felt freshly lit in an amber warmth. The master joined palms and bowed to the third student. "We bring the past with us. That is where we find our lineage. We include everything, the pleasant and the painful, the helpful and the harmful, in the journey of awakening. Bring it all with you. Leave nothing out of your experience. This is what allows for recognition of your true nature to arise. We compost our past lives until they become rich soil. Then — as we are bound by our vows to not replicate the atrocities of *samsara* — confidence will dawn. Do not worship me," the master raised a finger in warning, "for at the end of it all, I know nothing more than you do. Devote yourself to the path, and only the path."

The third student felt a bond begin to grow. The student couldn't tell if it this was self-confidence, or confidence in the teacher, or if the distinction even mattered. "Are you ready?"

The teacher said. The student and the teacher bowed to each other.

"Let's begin."

You Bring the Past with You

The above story is an expanded and reinterpreted version of a story from the Tibetan Buddhism tradition that I heard when I was younger.[1] I always love a good plot twist. I've contemplated the story many times since the Shambhala International organization fell apart in 2018. I realized that I — and many others — have lived versions of this story. Some of us have lived it many times over. The main, though not the only, cause of the collapse of Shambhala International was a reckoning over various abusive behaviors, boundary crossings, and at least one credible accusation of sexual assault against the head of the worldwide organization, Sakyong Mipham. I stepped down from my role in the New York organization soon after the allegations surfaced, but it took me longer to decide what to do about the formal guru-disciple relationship I had been in since 2002 with Sakyong Mipham, A few weeks before the first revelations of Sakyong Mipham's actions were made public, Eric Schneiderman, who had been a mentor to me in understanding the intersection between political engagement and spiritual practice, stepped down from his role as attorney general of New York State after a bombshell *New Yorker* article reported

---

1 The story is briefly mentioned in Chogyam Trungpa's *Cutting through Spiritual Materialism* and is sometimes attributed to the nineteenth-century Tibetan teacher Paltrul Rinpoche. A similar story exists in the Japanese Zen tradition.

a long-standing pattern of abuse in his romantic relationships. There was much to grapple with in 2018, and there has been more to grapple with ever since.

What happened in Shambhala International is not unique in the modern Buddhist world, or the larger world of spirituality. In his book *Love and Rage*, Lama Rod Owens describes his process of grappling with the fact that his guru both "saved my life" and caused a lot of harm. As I write this chapter, the spiritual world is grappling with the recent moment involving the eighty-seven-year-old Dalai Lama after a young boy in India requested a hug from him. The Dalai Lama embraced the boy closely for a long time, kissed him on the mouth (which the boy didn't ask for), and then (depending on the interpretation of the video of the incident) told the boy to either "bite" or "suck" his tongue.[2]

The "guru" relationship is unlike any other relationship with a teacher, precisely because it includes a committed vow between teacher and student. To be honest, I still can't say I understand this commitment well, even though I took a vow to a guru for seventeen years. Unlike any other form of student-teacher relationship, officially taking on a guru in Tantric

2 While this incident also demonstrated the power of social media to circulate and manipulate content, it was important for discussing the power dynamics of spiritual relationships. Having watched the unedited video, I wish the Dalai Lama had showed up and addressed the boy's family directly. He might've hosted a public forum where he acknowledges what the event brings up for people struggling to trust spiritual leaders and older men. Showing up after causing hurt, being present for accountability and repair, is everything. Otherwise everyone is left to process the event by themselves (usually via online forums, which are decidedly problematic spaces for heartfelt exchanges). These absences don't allow for healing and repair. The Dalai Lama's tepid indirect apology, sent through representatives, combined with other recent events and with his absence from the repair process, demonstrate the sort of disconnect that tends to increase distrust in spiritual leaders.

Buddhism requires taking the vow of *samaya* (literally, word of honor), which creates an unbreakable bond between the guru and the disciple.[3] More important than the bond with the specific human teacher, *samaya* creates an unbreakable bond between and the student's inherent awakened nature and the human lineage that transmits the direct experience of that awakened heart and mind. One widely misunderstood aspect of this commitment is that it rarely includes a close personal relationship with the guru. However, it does position the guru as the human center of the student's experience of the streams of wisdom teachings coming from the lineage that the person represents.

People are often surprised to hear that I hardly knew Sakyong Mipham at all, at least not personally. This was also true of the vast majority of those who had taken the *samaya* vow with him. My main way of knowing Sakyong Mipham as a teacher was to attend annual retreats with about 150 to 200 other Tantric students. At these retreats, we'd hear glowing, almost hagiographic stories of his latest activities, recited by his most trusted assistants. He gave deeply insightful lectures and guided-practice instructions that shaped my daily meditation practice for the coming year. These lectures and the retreats were almost always helpful in my own practice and life. Every once in a while, at the end of a large gathering like this, I was invited to a more intimate gathering with him, usually with other younger leaders in the community.

---

3 The word *guru* (like *Zen*, for that matter) is wildly misused in popular culture. In the Tantric Buddhist tradition, it is used only to refer to a teacher with whom a student has taken the vow of *samaya*. In that system, if both parties have not taken this vow to each other, then using the word *guru* is inappropriate.

Because Sakyong Mipham had so many disciples and face time with him was at a premium, these invitations were considered an honor. But these more intimate gatherings — ten or so people around a dinner table with Sakyong Mipham — were almost always uneasy and stilted. People were eggshell-level polite and would usually try to praise Sakyong Mipham as much as they could. The assembled guests rarely had meaningful conversations about ourselves, our community, or the world. Sakyong Mipham grew visibly uneasy if the conversation got away from him or from praise for his work, but he was also too quiet and shy to steer the conversation in the direction he wanted it to go. Simply put, it was just awkward.

Here's the dissonance that I'll work to understand for the rest of my life: when I studied the philosophies of the mind and practiced the contemplative techniques that were taught in Shambhala, I felt more confident, more grounded, kinder, and more authentic. But in the rare moments when I spent time close to the central teacher of our global organization, or when I tried to understand my place within the many constructed and rigid organizational hierarchies, I felt decidedly more performative, more insecure, and less authentic. Sometimes the whole thing felt like a festival of fragilities. I doubt I will ever fully reconcile this contradiction. Perhaps that is the lesson.

Commitment to a guru has to do with offering ourselves a stable yet safe container in which to work with ambivalence, that wishy-washy relationship humans can have to embracing a path. You can have all sorts of experiences in a committed relationship, and the commitment itself offers a container for learning from the full array of feelings without running away. When that commitment is mutual and consensual and has appropriate boundaries, it can be a powerful aid to awakening. But on the flip side, worship can lead to a cult of personality in which everyone is encouraged to pay more attention to the guru than to themselves or each other. Such communities are glued together by a perception of the leader's greatness, not by the strength of community itself. If you've ever watched a Trump rally, you know the worst version of this style of confusion. The man on stage talks endlessly about himself and his grievances, and the crowd somehow thinks his complaints have something to offer them. The individuals in the audience seem completely irrelevant to the man with the microphone. As long as there are warm bodies in the crowd, he has everything he needs.

In I'm not comparing my former guru to the former president. Sakyong Mipham was far more shy, almost boyish in public, and I believe he was trying to do good. His narcissistic insecurities, to the degree that they could be seen publicly, felt less malignant than those of #45. Yet he always needed to remain the center of attention, and we were expected to treat him as a faultless wisdom being, when clearly he had his own emotional baggage. I'm not sure he even knew a person who hadn't taken a vow to him as the guru. which can only warp a person's sense of who they are. It seemed impossible for him to receive much — if any — real feedback. Because he had no peers who could look him in the eye, he struck me as a lonely man. For me, the Shambhala organization felt most "awakened" in his absence, on my visits to local centers with strong communities. Those trips felt like going to a beloved cousin's house and enjoying your time there. It wasn't quite *my* house, but it was family, nonetheless. When people gathered at local centers, spending time with mentors and elders, yes, but mostly with each other, that's when I saw little glimpses of what we were supposed to be pursuing all along: this thing called "enlightened society."

After I stepped down from my official role in the organization, I contemplated the subtleties of my own immature grasping for advancement within the hierarchy (which, to be fair to myself, seemed structurally designed to keep a person grasping), and the way these tendencies had caused me to enable confusion and harm. I also considered what to do about my *saṃaya* vow. Taking on a guru is the only student-teacher relationship that involves this lifelong vow. I didn't want to end this deep and serious commitment without some attempt at a personal conversation with the man with whom I had made the vow.

I knew that any attempt at such communication was likely to fail. Sakyong Mipham had made only two vague public statements since the harms came to light, statements that seemed as much written by a lawyer as by him. By all reports from those who had been close to him, he wasn't talking to anyone. This withdrawal, the failure of a powerful person to be present for accountability and repair, seems to be typical of communities where such harms have occurred. Months after everything came to the surface, I wrote Sakyong Mipham a letter, requesting to discuss our *samaya* vow (in truth, it was not only my vow to him but our vow to each other). I received confirmation that this letter was handed to him personally. As expected, there was no response. Despite my sadness, I was relieved that he didn't answer. For me, the lack of response signaled that he was making the choice for both of us, that any mutual obligation was dissolved. In light of all that had happened, it felt exceedingly straightforward to let go of a relationship that wasn't one.

Just like the students in the classic Tibetan story, I moved on from that teacher. I had never bought into the idea that a person must have one teacher who stands above the rest. For a philosophical system that speaks repeatedly about the interdependence of all beings, the idea that you choose one being to serve as your only source of wisdom felt deeply antithetical to the teachings themselves. Even within Shambhala, I had multiple relationships with mentors and teachers that were a lot closer and more meaningful than my relationship with Sakyong Mipham. I studied with and read the works of various Buddhist teachers outside Shambhala. I also explored a lot of wisdom traditions that weren't officially Buddhist at all, including Western psychology. In Buddhist terms, my therapist is one of my crucial teachers.

I still fully consider myself a student of Tantric Buddhism, and I am in active relationship with a teacher of that tradition. I am not sure I'll ever refer to someone as my guru. Some people have a much stronger sense of heart opening and singular devotion when they meet that *one* teacher. I deeply support them in that experience. There are so many paths. But my own connection to teachers and lineage has always been a complex and interwoven experience, and I wasn't ever much use to anyone when it came to pretending otherwise.

Sometimes we focus solely on the frustrations, harms, and disappointments of the past. Our minds are more easily hooked by harmful actions than by examples of growth or wisdom. Admittedly, I don't believe I carry direct harm or any capital-T trauma from what happened in Shambhala. Therefore it was easier for me to work to integrate the complex lessons of my past into what came next. The process of moving on was hard enough for me. For somebody who has experienced trauma or abuse, it can be a thousand times harder. Still, if we step back for a moment from focusing on the harm, we can take the opportunity to reexamine what it means to be part of a spiritual lineage, of a human lineage.

Lineage is inherently supportive. Your lineage helps you discover your own power. From this perspective, this larger cultural moment presents a genuine opportunity to develop a more complex, balanced, and healthy relationship to tradition and hierarchies in general. The thoughtful reinterpretation of tradition and hierarchy can be a real gift in a moment when it feels like so much is falling apart in the world.

It's a wonderful thing that we are having deep and meaningful reexaminations of communal structures and student-teacher relationships in Buddhist and other spiritual traditions. Anybody who grows defensive about these conversations about power (and sadly people often do, including myself) needs to remember that being a guide or a teacher — and certainly a "guru" — is never a guaranteed status, and just like any other position, it's never permanent. *Teacher* is a role, not an identity. Being a guide — in any tradition — is a role that an elder practitioner enters willingly, with the agreement of the student. Guiding someone else is a job that should last only as long as both parties agree. Not only does the student have to consent to becoming a student, but the teacher must also agree to becoming that student's teacher.[4] The relationship can — and

4 For this reason, I am not personally a fan of referring to someone as your "teacher" if you've never met them, or if they have not consented to teaching you in some fashion. Many people refer to inspiring spiritual authors — or even people who passed away long ago — as their teacher. But I prefer to preserve the term for those guides with whom we've been in some ongoing relationship of practice and study where roles and duties have been laid out clearly for both parties.

should — dissolve when it's no longer useful. When a teaching relationship incorporates clear, healthy boundaries and mutual respect, a wisdom lineage can flourish and be flexible enough to sustain itself in the long term.

Similar reexaminations of hierarchy are going on all over the place, from labor strikes to political movements for empowerment to the interrogation of the student-teacher relationship across many academic fields of study. Sometimes these conversations come out of revelations of hurt and harm. Sometimes these interrogations of power come from a grassroots uprising against constructs that don't make a lot of sense. Sometimes they include an adolescent rebelliousness that may feel immature and judgmental, but which is a necessary part of any dialogue on how to reduce future suffering.

These processes can be frustrating and messy. For example, I know many people who teach at art schools. Just like Buddhism, art is a practice that has many traditions and forms of wisdom transmission. To study art is to immerse oneself in a long, rich lineage, and from a Buddhist perspective, an art teacher is a holder of that lineage. I asked one friend, a longtime professor at an elite art institution, how it was going. "Teaching is *terrible* right now," she said, laughing in both frustration and appreciation. "The students don't even want to be *taught* anymore. I want to lean over and say to them, 'Why are you even spending all this money on art school? Why not just save the money and go *be* an artist, if you don't want to be taught?'" Similar stories come from almost everyone I know who teaches in academia.

I'm a big fan of people holding their seat and claiming their power, because that's what the practice of confidence is all about. Students have power, especially in high-priced educational institutions where the relationship between the student and institution is sometimes as much a transaction of status and money as it is a transmission of knowledge and wisdom. To claim power as a student means to hold your seat, know what you need, and leverage that power for a given purpose. When you step into the study of any lineage — whether spiritual, psychological, artistic, cultural, or political — you see that some previous modes of thought and behavior have become sanctified when really they're just shared habits of previous generations that nobody has adequately questioned. Hence the phrase "OK, Boomer."[5] Buddhist tradition contains many such constructs, academia contains them, and electoral politics and journalism are up to their eyeballs in them.

At the same time, to be part of a lineage involves humility, the realization that none of us can learn what we need to know all by ourselves. Balancing the empowerment of the student (which is, ultimately, the only reason for teaching) with the integrity of the lineage and respect for those who came before is a dynamic, push-pull process. And it's a balance we're all figuring out as we go.

The Confidence That Comes from Lineage

Power and confidence are derived interdependently. Confidence is not something any of us can generate alone. If you have a good support structure, then confidence arises naturally. One helpful way to define it is this: Confidence is the

5 I can't wait to see what dismissive phrase "Gen Alpha" comes up with for my generation as we age.

internalization of the support structure that reminds you that you're capable. Human examples of the qualities you want to bring out in yourself can mirror your own strength and bravery. Think of one teacher, mentor, or ancestor who reminds you of your own strength or bravery. Who comes to mind? How do you feel when you hold this person in your heart right now? Do you feel connected? Do you feel supported? Do you feel capable?

In Tantric Buddhism, lineage is represented as a great tree with many branches. Lineage is much more than our spiritual heritage. It includes every source of wisdom, bravery, and love we've known. It includes the spiritual teachings we've received and those who have passed them on, along with the heroic figures of any other traditions of wisdom — such as psychology, art, or social justice — that we've received and carry with us. It also includes our familial and cultural ancestries. We have each had meaningful teachers and heroic figures in whatever work we might be doing in the world. We are all the inheritors of the blessing of those who came before. You are not alone; you are not the first person to try to figure this all out; nor will you be the last. You don't have to make anything up, and in fact you can't really make anything up, because nobody creates anything alone.

However, lineage doesn't always feel supportive. Sometimes contemplating lineage brings feelings of inadequacy or shame. Buddhists should never overlook the problems that have been present in both ancient and modern Buddhism. In *Buddhism after Patriarchy*, the scholar Rita Gross examines the sexism inherent in Buddhist hierarchies that date back to the time of Siddhartha Gautama. She notes Gautama's reluctance to allow women to join the monastic community and their treatment as second-class citizens when they were finally admitted. Gross looks for ways that Buddhism can move on from its patriarchal history.

Patriarchal arrangements of community are not the only problems in Buddhism. Whenever I read a contemporary article about the "militant" Buddhist voices in Myanmar (Burma), I want to hide. What, in the ever-loving hell, I wonder, is militant Buddhism? And I still have some issues with Siddhartha Gautama. I suspect that his propensity to avoid the world and its social relations may have set Buddhism on a course that has encouraged turning away from life in society. Yet its traditions of mindfulness and contemplative practice hold great potential for influencing society. I frequently wrestle with — and feel grateful but ambivalent toward — the wise-but-avoidant personas of my tradition. You could reasonably claim that Buddhism has navigated its long history with less strife and violence than other spiritual traditions, but some historians argue convincingly that this tradition is just as dysfunctional as any other. Either way, over the long course of its history, Buddhism has had its own versions of the same problems that all human traditions have faced.

There's a possible perception that invoking one's ancestors should be a supportive act, and that one's ancestral lineage is always loving, brave, and wise. Yet many of us have complex or downright harmful associations with our family lineages. This is especially true for people who come from abusive homes. It's also true for people of privilege whose ancestors engaged in harmful practices to earn status, wealth, and power. Recently, I interviewed the author and Zen teacher Zenju Earthlyn

Manuel. Osho Zenju is a fascinating figure when it comes to holding multiple lineages. In her book *The Shamanic Bones of Zen*, she reexamines the ceremonial and shamanic roots of her Japanese Buddhist lineage and finds many themes of ancestry and shamanism similar to the ones that she found in the Black church of her childhood. As I read her book and spoke with Osho Zenju, I pondered how Buddhist teachings ceremonially invoke the presence of lineage, and how various traditional wisdom streams make use of ancestor practices.

But is the past always there to support you? I asked Osho Zenju about the often complicated relationship we have to our ancestries. I was thinking of my own Buddhist lineage and family history as well as of my friend Maud Newton's great book *Ancestor Trouble*, where she reckons with the discovery that her Southern ancestors were slaveholders.[6] Not all of our inheritance feels wise or good.

"You carry it *all* with you," Osho Zenju said. "Not just the good." She spoke of a Zen practice of chanting the names of the teachers who came before, and of once wishing she could simply skip, omit, or cross out certain names on the list, but realizing it was impossible to do so. I knew that feeling well.

One person who always comes to mind when I invoke the brilliant complexity of my own lineage is my Grandma Claire. One of the first successful women producers of Broadway plays, she was a fierce, powerful trailblazer. Claire was also a wonderful grandmother. She would hold her seat regally, relaxing in her Eames-style 1970s leather recliner, a seat of power that earned her the family nickname Chair. She directed the

6 I have recently learned, through a cousin's diligent research, that it's quite likely that one of my own Southern ancestors was also a slaveholder.

family's traffic from that seat, giving the rest of us directions with an authentic boldness that made it impossible to refuse her wishes. She was by far my closest grandparent. I lost her when I was about sixteen, as I was moving toward adulthood and needed the blessing of her confidence. Sometimes now I imagine myself having conversations with her about a difficult decision or a fear of doing something hard. Grandma Claire is a daring force in my heart, and when I invoke her in my visualizations of lineage, I reconnect with my ancestral bravery.

At the same time, there's a consensus in the family that Grandma Claire probably suffered from undiagnosed bipolar disorder. I was shielded from witnessing her depressive and manic episodes, but she attempted suicide on multiple occasions. It also seems that when my aunt was born, Claire walked straight out of the hospital after the birth, simply forgetting to take her newborn daughter with her. (Eventually, the story goes, she did return to the hospital for her child.) Was Claire a trailblazing creative? Was she a legendary grandmother? Was she far from the most secure presence as a mother? Yes.

Wouldn't it be nice if we could pick and choose the aspects of our lineage that we want to influence us? If we could purify our histories and separate the healthy inheritances from the harmful ones, the good eggs from the bad seeds, the wisdom from the confusion? If we could just throw those "trash" humans out of our heart, and hold onto the saints? Alas, lineage can be neither pasteurized nor homogenized. Of course we can connect internally with the figures who acted most bravely or decently, those who inspire us the most — and we definitely should bring those safe and beloved beings forward as much as possible in our awareness. But we can't "move on" from our lineage, because our historical inheritance is woven into us. It might be updated, changed, or transformed, but it can't be erased. Whether we acknowledge it or not, whether we want to or not, we carry our lineage with us. You can decide to take time out from talking to your parents, for example, but you can't fire them from being your parents. You can break up, but you can't say a relationship doesn't continue to shape you.

History is a mess. This is true of every society, every family, and every lineage. It's especially true for the American lineage, a society that was built on twin horrors: the genocide of Indigenous peoples and brutal slavery. We are now a multiracial family of hundreds of millions of people that still hasn't properly reckoned with our family history. We long for the wisdom that would enable us to create a society that doesn't replicate those harmful systems. But any future society will be crafted out of the same flawed human material from which those confused systems evolved. There's no way to burn it all down without scorching ourselves in the process. It would be like trying to incinerate our spiritual DNA. We are here now because they were there then. That's how causality works.

When we're feeling disheartened, we tend to look at our lineages as if regarding a pile of human garbage. But when we're looking clearly, we see them as a worthy and sacred mess. And that's what we are, too. In all our messy complexity, we find the raw ingredients of awakened humanity. We find the worthiness to take our seats. We are worthy. Ironically, that's something Sakyong Mipham used to say a lot.

Just as we do when examining ourselves, we need to develop as much honesty as we can muster about the lineages that we've come from. To do this requires a willingness to look critically as well as to be open to criticism about the blind spots in our understanding of history. Sometimes people who haven't seen my various public statements ask if I'm still "involved" in Shambhala. Here's my answer: "If you mean the Shambhala International organization, I stepped down from my role in 2018. I have no involvement at this time. If you mean my *samaya* vow with Sakyong Mipham, then that commitment was dissolved by mutual agreement in early 2019. But if you wonder whether or not the Shambhala teachings and lineage are still a part of me, that's not even a choice I could make if I wanted to. The answer will always be yes."

The Lineage Tree

Here's a visualization practice to invoke the power and confidence of your personal lineage. Visualization can allow your meditation to become more creative and personal. In this exercise you create the mental space to contemplate — and draw strength from — your internal support structure.

This practice comes from a classic Tantric representation for lineage called the Jewel Tree, Lineage Tree, or Refuge Tree.[7] The representation of lineage as a massive tree conveys the interconnections among past, present, and future. Trees are also a timeless way to describe the structure of a large family. Tibetan *thangka* paintings often depict a particular historical lineage of Tibetan Buddhism as a tree. In the main trunk of the tree there is usually an archetype who represents the awakened mind.

7 The visualization is derived from the practices of the seventh-century Indian teacher Shantideva, with modern instructions by Robert Thurman, Joe Loizzo, and Miles Neale.

This central representation of wisdom is surrounded by heroic figures, teachers, guides, ancestors, and protective beings from that particular lineage. This complex imagery is often invoked in classic devotional practices. Traditionally, the meditator prostrates themself to the assembled beings in order to connect with the power and blessings of that lineage. When you look at the painting of a particular teaching lineage, you may feel strongly connected to certain members of the group and not so connected to others. As Osho Zenju said, you might even want to cross out certain figures in the painting.

When I was younger, I worked intensely with this kind of devotional practice related to the classic depictions of the Tantric Buddhist lineage. In fact, I did a couple hundred thousand prostrations to the Tantric Buddhist lineage. It was a practice that helped me let go of feeling so isolated in the universe and honor the great intelligence I had inherited. Over the years I've come to view it as a way to map and recall a personally defined lineage. We each have our own lineage tree; no two are the same. The beings and images we envision are unique to each of us. Thus, in the Jewel Tree meditation, I now allow myself much more space to be curious about which ancestors, heroes, and teachers appear when I invoke the lineage.

Feel free to read through this imaginative meditation slowly. Take time to feel your way through each step. Allow at least fifteen minutes, but be aware that it might take thirty minutes or more. With visualization meditation, don't ever worry about painting a perfect picture. It's not an exercise it draftsmanship, it's a way to feel connective support with the most awakened qualities of our ancestors. Allow the visualization to spark any emotional connection that might be meaningful to you. The key is to contemplate and deepen your personal connection to your lineages, not to follow someone else's definition.

Sit for a few minutes, either on a chair or on a cushion, but take a posture where you can rest your body in relative stillness, where you feel like you can fully take your seat. You might scan your body or connect with your breath for a few minutes to gather and settle.

Imagine yourself sitting in a meadow on a warm, breezy spring day. In front of you is a massive tree with huge branches and leafy boughs that could support the weight of many, many ancestors. The roots of this tree reach so far down into the soil that they form a nourishing interchange with the entire planet, intermingling with all other root systems. This deep foundation makes the tree an immovable entity that no storm or wind could ever fell. In the center of the great tree is a being who represents the deepest aspirations for your life, such as wisdom, love, and compassion. This could be an iconic figure, like Jesus or Gautama Buddha. It could be a personal teacher of yours, if you have one main spiritual teacher. It could be a heroic figure with whom you feel a deep connection. Or it could be a not-quite-human spiritual archetype like a bodhisattva or saint.[8] If you can't think of one single central figure, then invite several. See who shows up.

Next, invite any other teachers or significant figures from any spiritual lineages to which you feel a connection. Let them take their seats in the lush, emerald boughs of the tree.

8 For the central figure in my Jewel Tree visualization I often use the nonhuman bodhisattva called Tara (or Dolma), an archetype who takes different forms depending on the particular wise energy needed in a given situation.

Now, invite your familial ancestors. Start with the ancestors you feel most loved and supported by. Call on the ancestors who give you confidence and a general feeling of warmth and worthiness. If an ancestor shows up whose history is more complex, see if you can make space for them, too. But if someone from your lineage shows up with whom you only have harmful or even abusive associations, it's fine to shift your focus away from them, or simply say, "Not now."

Now, invite the heroic ancestors of the work you're doing in the world, and any cultural heroes you want to invoke. Every field of knowledge has its own wisdom holders and a lineage to be honored and invoked. If you're working on political activism, invite heroic organizers. If you're a cook, invite great chefs. Whatever you're trying to do in this world — and especially if you're struggling with a particular aspect of that work — invoke the wisdom holders of that tradition to come and offer support. In particular, invite those ancestors and cultural heroes who manifest the qualities you are trying to evoke. See who shows up, and allow them to take their seats.

Finally, you can imagine around you the truth (dharma) protectors. Protector beings are any beings (human, ethereal, or other) who guard your path from outer harm, but they also keep you internally honest when ego insecurity, fragility, and arrogance arise. Dharma protectors protect you from the world, and they also protect you from yourself. If any such protective beings come to mind, invite them to take a place in the tree or to join the outer perimeter of the visualization.

With the guests present, first imagine yourself bowing to all the assembled wisdom beings. This is not an act of subservience but rather a gesture of gratitude and respect. You can show gratitude that you're not alone in this human mess, that you don't have to discover wisdom all by yourself.

Second, sometimes these acts of gratitude are accompanied by making offerings to your lineage that you place on the tree, like flowers or gifts, or anything else you imagine yourself placing on the tree. You may also place offerings like candles, incense, or flowers to your personal lineage on your shrine or altar. Take a few minutes to feel included and supported by your lineage, to rest in the imaginative setting, feeling mutual warmth and care. See how the support makes you feel.

Third, rejoice. Rejoicing means taking time to celebrate your own positive qualities. This is your chance to contemplate what you're doing well in your work, practice, or relationships. What positive qualities or successes have you been growing and building on recently? If nothing positive about your recent efforts comes to mind, please think again. If still no positive qualities come to mind, at least rejoice in your ability to show up and try, both in this practice session and in life in general. Notice how hard it can be to acknowledge your own strengths and wise qualities. As you celebrate your growth, feel the lineage rejoicing with you and cheering you on.

Fourth, you can disclose whatever difficulties or obstacles you're struggling with. *Where am I stuck?* Feel the support of the lineage, and remind yourself that many others have struggled similarly. Notice whether any of the assembled figures can speak directly to your struggle from their own lived example. If you're struggling with anxiety or trying to develop bravery to do something that is difficult for you, for example, you're far from the first member of your lineage to struggle that way. Whom can you call on for help?

Fifth, request your lineage, ancestors, and heroic figures to be with you and support you on your journey, day and night. If you want, at this point you can spend a few minutes reciting a mantra that has meaning for you; reciting a phrase of loving-kindness such as "May I be brave," "May I be at ease," or "May all beings be free from suffering"; or expressing specific support for what's coming up for you.

Sixth, ask the figures of your lineage to remain with you, manifesting their bravery, skill, and kindness, as you proceed with the work. Then imagine the outer edges of the meadow and tree dissolving into light. You can imagine all the beings dissolving into a soft, powerful light (like moonlight) and collecting in the central figure or figures of your visualization. Then imagine that figure or figures dissolving into the same light. Feel that light gently pouring into your heart center. The lineage lives within you. Because your connection with all these beings is conjured by your own mind, they are never really separate from you.

Seventh (the final step), rest for a few minutes, feeling protected, supported, and empowered with the qualities you are seeking to cultivate. Then imagine how you might use your own wisdom for the aid and benefit of sentient beings, including — but not only — yourself. Let yourself rest mindfully for a final few moments in the feeling of being supported. You can close, if you like, by dedicating the merit, which is the traditional practice of acknowledging your own effort and wishing that whatever benefit may come from your practice and work in the world will spread and grow.

CHAPTER EIGHT

The Power of Awareness

Awareness is the body of meditation, as is taught.
Whatever arises is fresh — the essence of realization.

— Mahāmudrā (Kagyu lineage) meditation chant

I come to consciousness in the back of the ambulance. This is the third time this has happened to me in the past year or so, but this time the disorientation is worse. The last time, I came to consciousness in my apartment and lay down on the stretcher myself. But this time it takes longer to regain my sense of being me — to reinhabit the control tower at the center of my world. In the back of the ambulance, I feel the male EMT staring at me with anger and frustration, while the female EMT is looking at me forgivingly. I don't know why this man is mad at me, but it doesn't take long to figure out that I had another grand mal seizure. Like the other two this year, it happened in bed, while I was asleep.

Soon after this, I see a seizure specialist who prescribes the right dose of the right medicine, and from that time until almost four years later, as I'm writing these words, I won't have a single seizure. I will soon learn, via another round of brain tests, that my epileptic activity occurs only in my sleep state. This is a blessing for living my life functionally — in bed is the safest place to have a seizure — but it's also a curse for my awareness, as well as for the piece of me that likes to maintain the myth of control over my body and actions. I won't get many answers about what caused the seizures, or why I suddenly developed epilepsy in my late thirties. I also won't gain any real awareness of what a grand mal seizure feels like. While there were a few minor "auras," or mini-seizures, in the years before the grand mal ones (thirty- to forty-five-second spans where I lost my grasp on language while in conversation with someone), my awareness wasn't present at all during these large seizures. The only perceptual footprints of my seizures are lingering muscle soreness and the place where I bit my own tongue, which takes several days to heal. I know of the events themselves only from what observers mirror back to me afterward. I know my seizures were terrifying to watch.

After the physical convulsions end, seizures often include a period called the postictal state. During this period, someone who just had an epileptic convulsion can appear to be awake and acting somewhat intentionally, but they aren't. In fact, the early origins of the term *lunatic* arose from the mistaken connection between the full moon (*luna*) and epileptic seizures. For twenty to thirty minutes after my convulsions ended, I was apparently acting very unlike a person who has been meditating for twenty-five years. I called out for my mother and also addressed other people in the room as Mom, including my (now-ex-) wife (what's up, Dr. Freud?). I stumbled around our apartment muttering to myself and ignored the terrified cries of my daughter (then two years old), a person whose tears would normally grab my full attention the instant her ducts began to moisten. Meanwhile, my wife was trying to figure out how to keep me from hurting myself in my state. When the EMTs arrived, I reacted like they were predators chasing me, rather than two people there to help. I slammed the bedroom door closed and hid under the bedcovers. When the EMT entered and tried to grab my arm to transfer me to the stretcher, I bit her wrist.

A seizure — as my specialist later explained to me — is like an electrical storm in the brain that causes a reboot. The part of the network that reboots first, it seems, is the limbic system, which controls our earliest evolutionary response to threats: freezing, fleeing, or fighting without considering the situation in context. For the first time in my adult life, I had the humbling experience of looking like I was awake, but having no recognition for any of my actions. This Buddhist guy was pure amygdala, a goblin of *samsara*.

You can wax poetic only about that which happens to you in a state of awareness. What happens when you are neither awake nor dreaming is much harder to describe. The loss of consciousness has happened to many of us who practice mindfulness. It happens to all of us every day, when we fall asleep. Buddhist teachings include ways to investigate the awareness of dreams, to gain further confidence in your sense of knowing that the present is accessible even in states of subtle consciousness and unconsciousness. After a grand mal seizure, you get the special gift of a period of time where — to an external observer — you look awake, but you most certainly don't act like it.

When I wrote *The Road Home*, I told the brief story of connecting with my spacious awareness on a sleepless red-eye flight, holding my seat with the sadness and beauty of being human, finding open-heartedness in the midst of heartbreak. It was a decidedly triumphant moment of coming into awareness and creating space for what I was feeling. More than any other point in that book, readers have told me that this simple story resonated with them. One of the central premises of Buddhist thought is the idea that an unconditional aspect of awareness is always present, a spacious sense of knowing that operates under all our confused thoughts and mental chatter, all our anxiety, fantasy, and frustrations. It's an aspect of awareness that persists no matter what emotional state we're in, no matter what dramas we're fixating on, no matter what our current level of "cray" may be. The moment of recognizing that I was in the ambulance, that I had just had another seizure, was also a moment of awareness. You could say that it was the beginning of coming back to the present moment after an unusually violent period of absence. But this awareness didn't feel like a triumph. It felt like humiliation.

In his movie *Fierce Grace*, the now-departed Ram Dass describes how having a life-altering stroke humbled him. He questioned his ability to navigate what heart and mind would do when life really fell apart. He said, "I'm supposed to be Mr. Spiritual, and I failed the test." My grand mal seizures were not nearly as disruptive to my cognitive functioning in the long term as Ram Dass's stroke. Beyond the slow march of aging — the understandable need for an extra moment to remember random facts now and again — my day-to-day brain function hasn't changed much. But those stories of my actions in the postical state — the image of me fending off people who were there to help me, like a little boy stumbling through the trenches of an imaginary war zone — don't reflect how I imagine handling difficult moments after twenty-five years of meditation practice. The event gave me much to contemplate about how much our consciousness is tied to our nervous systems, the layers of our brains, and the constraints of our evolution.

The Shame of Becoming Aware

Coming to awareness isn't always pleasant, even if it eventually leads in a helpful direction. Initial moments of clear seeing aren't always eureka moments, some shining halo of insight. Moments of initial awareness are usually painful precisely because of the disorientation that comes with the recognition that we've previously been unconscious. In a broader sense, this is what's happening in our world right now as we contemplate centuries-old systems of confusion. The recognition of a blind spot can be shocking and induce defensiveness. It's embarrassing to realize you've been in zombie mode. Obviously, returning to awareness after each of my seizures was distressing because I had been so out of control of what my physical body did, and because there was a period when other people perceived me as conscious — and therefore, accountable — when I was not at all. The dawn of recognition in the ambulance felt like reclaiming myself from a body snatcher. And what did the body snatcher do with — and to — my body? Why did this electrical storm happen again inside my skull? What the fuck is wrong with you, Brain? What's wrong with *me*?

Sometimes the dawn of recognition feels like waking up

after a night out drinking, that sense of "Oh, no, what did I do last night?" Awakening from this level of ignorance is shocking. In his book *Penetrating Wisdom: The Aspiration of Samantabhadra*, my teacher Dzogchen Ponlop Rinpoche writes:

> There is a sense of terror that arises when you come out of unconsciousness. Sometimes we have the experience when we take a siesta, at least I have. It's a very weird experience to wake up from a long siesta in the afternoon. It's a kind of terror. You don't know exactly what time it is. You think it's morning, but, when you look, the sun is just setting or it is already dark. It's like going from that unconscious state to consciousness. There's always a mysterious experience in that very moment of switch.... [I]n the very moment of waking up you can feel that terror.

A triumphant story from ancient Buddhist history tells of the recovery of awareness but also depicts a moment of great shame and terror. King Ashoka lived approximately three hundred years after Siddhartha. He began his reign as a bloodthirsty tyrant. Ashoka led his armies into a savage war that ultimately delivered him conquest of the large region of Kalinga (now Orissa). I imagine Ashoka in his early days as being like Vladimir Putin, only more skilled and successful at warfare. As he surveyed the bodies piled on the battlefield, already feeling queasy about the carnage carried out in his name, Ashoka apparently caught sight of a Buddhist monk walking across the battlefield. The juxtaposition of the atrocities Ashoka had ordered and the gentle, unshakable demeanor of the monk led to a spark of awareness in Ashoka. It is said that from that moment of awareness, the tyrant Ashoka changed his course completely. He eventually became a Buddhist and a pacifist. He is also credited with creating some of the world's first veterinary hospitals. Ironically, it's likely because of Ashoka's territorial conquests that Buddhism spread much farther and faster through India and Southeast Asia. This is the rarest of all tales in this world: a powerful and aggressive man having a complete change of heart, becoming an agent of peace and humanitarianism. It rarely happens that way, but that's this story, at least.

The part of this tale that gets glossed over is Ashoka's grappling with shame. That moment of coming to awareness must have sparked very difficult feelings in the mighty king. As he ruled after his change of heart, Ashoka's various edicts were placed on pillars around his kingdom. One read, "His Majesty feels profound sorrow and regret" for the conquest of Kalinga. I imagine, in our modern parlance, that what Ashoka really felt was many years of compounded shame, a shame that he had to spend the rest of his life working through in one way or another.

This dawn of recognition — this moment of "Where have I been? What have I participated in?" — brings up a particular form of shame, which I'll call the shame of awareness. This is an experience we all have, and something those of us with privilege must go through if we're going to confront the world we've inherited and enabled. The shame associated with coming back to awareness is a problem that meditators experience all the time. When recognition comes back online (the moment we reawaken to present experience), we might celebrate the return to awareness. But instead, we usually feel shame that we lost presence so completely and for so long. In mindfulness meditation, whenever we come back to the present experience, we have the opportunity either to celebrate that we're back or to beat ourselves up for the fact that we were gone.

Sometimes the dawn of recognition conveys a sense of terror, as Ponlop Rinpoche says. Sometimes — especially when dealing with trauma — we have to gauge carefully how quickly we bring attention to the experiences of which we're becoming aware. For example, within an hour after each seizure, my body — albeit sore — was functioning well enough. I wasn't sick or injured. I could have left the emergency room and gone to work if I'd chosen to. But I needed some time to recover and integrate what had happened to me. Sometimes the recognition is so shocking that you want to push back in defensiveness against it. A part of me wanted to question my wife's narration of how I acted right after my seizure, because I had no memory of it and couldn't quite believe what she told me about my actions. In Buddhism, we are called upon to develop awareness that confused beliefs and patterns of behavior have been leading us through cycles of dissatisfaction for a very long time, maybe even lifetimes. There can be a tendency to push back defensively against this truth, rather than embrace the recognition immediately with warmth and care.

I notice this same pushback against awareness in the drive to ban materials in schools and libraries that convey an accurate depiction of American history. It's painful to watch white parents at school-board meetings demanding that certain novels, textbooks, and curricula for teaching American history be banned because they don't want their child to feel bad about being white.[1] First of all, this reaction involves tremendous overpersonalizing. Nobody is asking children to feel individual shame; they are asking them to build a healthy rapport with their own awareness of shared history. Second, when we deny our children the opportunity to look at painful truth head-on and integrate their feelings about it, we don't help those kids develop any tools for meeting shame, fear, and anger later on in life when they come to awareness about other difficult experiences, whether personal or collective. The curriculum "debate," if there really is one, transcends the question of which version of history is accurate. From a Buddhist perspective, when books are banned, kids are taught that awareness itself — which necessarily includes moments of shock and shame — is a bad thing. The emotional and spiritual damage involved in being told to suppress your awareness runs far deeper than a debate about whether a student should be reading book X or book Y.

The realization that some aspect of the truth scares or humbles you is one of most important moments in the development of the awakened mind. Coming back to awareness is necessary for what meditation teachers sometimes call a fresh start. We have to reframe our view to see that awareness is always a mark of progress and therefore is a basically good thing, even if the experience beheld by awareness provokes a difficult emotion. We have a habitual tendency to vilify ignorance, but we don't always celebrate awareness. I was humbled by my own brain and nervous system during my seizures. But the experience gave me much more awareness and compassion for myself

---

1 After much organized protest, Missouri school libraries removed Toni Morrison's classic debut novel, *The Bluest Eye,* from the banned list in 2022.

and others. The humiliation I felt was ultimately empowering, because it became humility. It empowered tenderness toward myself and compassion for everyone living in nervous systems and brains that don't always function perfectly.

The Space of Awareness

Awareness itself is ungraspable. It's not any particular experience; it's a space of knowing that contains every experience we have. Simply put, awareness is not a "thing." It can't be reified or turned into an object. It can't be dissected or analyzed in any sufficient way with words or symbols. Language is designed to point toward objects of experience rather than to describe the holder of experience itself. That witness or holder of experience is what we mean by the elusive word *awareness*. Certainly, as my seizures demonstrate, the ability to access awareness is embedded in the brain and body. There's no way around the body. If your physical hardware malfunctions, you lose track of that knowing quality of consciousness that says, "I am here, and this is happening. I can navigate this. I can recognize the moment and make an intentional decision." Modern science often (but not always) takes the mistaken view that consciousness can be completely reduced to activity in the brain. Neuroscientists believe conscious knowing is seated in the cerebral cortex (and that seems to be a good approximation of the physical "seat" of awareness), but these brain experiments are only external measures of enormously complex internal processes. The newer view is that awareness and brain function involve multiple networks — including the limbic system and the default mode network — rather than just one physical location.

Still, subjective humans are looking at the brain as an externalized object and trying to "find" awareness over "there," in "that" brain.

These mappings of conscious activity in the various arenas of the brain and body are likely to become increasingly nuanced and descriptive. But will object-based science ever be able to fully describe to us the what, where, and how of awareness? The underlying problem is that awareness itself isn't an object (or even a network) that can be found in an experiment. Awareness itself is holding space for the experiment we're performing. Awareness is neither substance nor location. Awareness is a space — a knowing, empty, and warm space.

For 2,500 years, Buddhist philosophers lacked adequate technology to look at the physical world with the same depth of "object-based" investigation that modern brain science delivers. The fact that physical science and contemplative science are now so much in conversation with each other may signal one of the greatest leaps forward in human well-being. What Buddhism has offered — hammered out in a shared, open-source technology over the millennia — is millions of practitioners subjectively verifying their experiences via countless internal experiments. Buddhist practitioners also spent those millennia conversing with all of the metaphysical philosophies the world has ever known. Buddhism developed tried-and-true experiments to discover what awareness is, how it operates, and where — if anywhere — it can be said to live.

When you go looking for awareness — either internally or externally — you ultimately can't find it. This is frustrating, but it's simple logic. You can't "find" your awareness because awareness is the entity that's looking! The classic teachings give the analogy of a person (without a mirror) trying to see their own eyeball. How would you see your eyeball if the eye is doing the looking? The eye (and the part of consciousness that relates to it) can know that it's seeing, can feel itself seeing, and can verify the phenomenon of sight, but it can't see the "seeing" as an object. In the same way, mind can't see mind (as the classic teachings say).

This is the first quality of awareness — it can't be perceived as an object or turned into a thing. The classic term for this aspect of awareness is "empty" (*shunya*), but that word can be a little confusing. Awareness is the empty space that holds all mental experience, rather than any experience that arises in that space.

Awareness can do two things. It can recognize itself through a reflexive sense of knowing, and it can behold whatever experiences arise in an accommodating manner. The power that comes from working with awareness is embedded in this second capacity, because it means that, as awareness grows more accustomed to recognizing itself, we can start to make room for any difficult experience. We can welcome any rough emotion, whether rage, shame, lust, or any other feeling that's hard to be with. Awareness, as that space-holder, is indestructible and unshakable.

In the classic meditations that take you deeper into the experience of awareness, you're not supposed to take anyone's word for this idea that awareness does not live in a specific place: you're supposed to test it out, again and again and again.[2] Instead of blind faith, you perform a contemplative experiment.

2 There are multiple traditions for investigating awareness. One such tradition in the Tantric teachings is known as *mahāmudrā* (meaning the great seal of reality).

You search for the location of consciousness again and again, in every way you could possibly find it. This is meant to be an exhaustive (and sometimes annoying) process, because you have to perform the experiment fully each time. Is awareness in my skull? (You might want to have a basic brain map to ask this question. The cortex is the uppermost and outer layer of the brain. Can you feel awareness there?) Is awareness in my heart center? Is it in my pelvic floor? My pinky toes? Is awareness dispersed throughout the body? If it is dispersed, then does awareness stop at the outer layer of my skin? Does awareness extend an inch outside the body? Is it my thoughts? My feelings? And on and on. And then a moment comes when the search is exhausted, and out of the exhaustion you relax a little bit, which feels like a mental sigh of relief, or as my father David says, like the moment after you decide to stop banging your head against a wall. After that relief, awareness settles into — and rests within — itself. This brief moment — which can gradually be prolonged with increased recognition — is akin to the moment that the eye stops looking for the eye, and instead relaxes into just *being* the eye, simply doing everything that an eye that trusts itself can do.

When awareness recognizes itself and relaxes into being what it is, it can hold space for any mental or bodily experience with clarity, in much the same way that the galaxy accommodates planets, stars, and meteors. When awareness recognizes itself, it's foolproof. Awareness never loses its seat, because it's the holder of *all* seats. Because we're not enlightened yet, and we generally haven't learned to recognize awareness and accommodate our own experience, this moment of awareness recognizing itself comes as a surprise, maybe even a shock.

When the arising experience is unthreatening, this surprise is something we appreciate, like saying "That's *it*!" But when the arising experience involves a difficult feeling (for example, the shame of realizing that you lost control of your body), it's much harder to settle into awareness. If you can tolerate the initial shock of having been absent from awareness, you start to witness even difficult feelings as welcome visitors to your mental home, visitors that arrive, stay a while, and then dissolve back into that knowing space of awareness.

With the confidence that awareness is more spacious than any experience that might arise within it, we can (eventually) come to view even the hardest experiences with curiosity. Anger, jealousy, shame, and anxiety can all become meaningful objects floating through the galaxy of awareness. There's more than enough room for all the feels, as the kids like to say. With awareness, even shame isn't a problem. Yes, shame requires reflection. Sometimes a shameful moment requires remorse and a reparatory action, but the arising of the shameful experience itself doesn't need to undercut your confidence.[3] Ultimate confidence comes from awareness recognizing itself. That's when you can start holding your seat, no matter what's going on.

The Warmth of Awareness

It is said that the knowing quality of awareness is spacious and empty, but it's also "luminous." Luminosity is a very interesting word. It means that when awareness recognizes itself, the experiences that arise become vivid and bright, and your mind itself

3 I couldn't get the name of the EMT I bit, so apology and repair weren't possible in my story.

also has a bright quality in addition to its openness. Because awareness is alive and knowing, it even has a sense of warmth toward experience, and this warmth is at the root of feeling love and connection. You might ask, Isn't awareness completely neutral, the way a mirror just reflects exactly what it receives? Don't words like *warmth* and *luminosity* display a kind of bias or judgment in a certain direction? Why be so optimistic about the whole thing? In the knowing space of awareness, there is curiosity, a kind of care toward existence itself. There's an appreciation for whatever happens. That doesn't render shame, fear, or heartbreak less painful, but it does make those difficult experiences less problematic. Everything that visits awareness is a guest — a warmly welcomed, vivid, and intriguing guest.

Leaning Back in Awareness

When we're on the meditation seat, we usually focus on trying to track the objects of experience, like the breath, for example. The mind has a tendency to get caught up in what I call "leaning forward." Leaning forward is the subtlest way to lose your seat. Leaning forward isn't about posture. It happens when you become overly vigilant about the object of your experience (the breath, a sound, a feeling or thought…your smartphone…). When you focus too hard on any object, you tend to want to either chase the experience or push it away. Following the breath is the best example of this tendency in formal meditation. Because people who meditate tend to think that paying attention to the breath means you're "good" at mindfulness (the same way a darts player would feel skilled if the dart hit the bullseye or a triple twenty, or at least the board), the mind tends to lean forward and try to chase after the breath. When you lean forward, chasing the experience, your brow furrows, and your mind and body tend to tense up a bit. Then, when you're unsuccessful at this hunt, you might want to rebel against the practice session, because the whole exercise feels stressful and deflating. You push the whole thing away in frustration and space out into fantasy, or else just say, as your skin crawls, "When is this gonna be over?"

It's the same way you might feel when you're really trying to pay attention to a movie in a theater. Your mind leans toward the action, trying to follow what's happening on the screen and immerse yourself in it. If the plot is engrossing, it's easy. But if the movie has slow parts or a convoluted story (*Wait, how does she know that guy again?*), your mind tends to rebel and space out, and you might even sneak a look at the time on your phone. Either way, you're struggling.

The alternative is to try leaning back.[4] What I mean by *lean back* is that you let your consciousness get more panoramic and spacious, rather than focused and invested. You notice the entire context of the movie: how the shot is framed on the screen, the theater itself, the audience, and most importantly, the projection of the film onto the screen. And at the same time, you relax into observing the movie, rather than chasing it. Leaning back is about settling fully into your movie seat, allowing the mind to relax and be more present with the *context* of your experience (awareness), rather than focusing on the *content* of experience (the current sense perception or thought). A classic

4 If your practice is truly advanced, you may hear the 2004 rap song "Lean Back" by Terror Squad, featuring Fat Joe, at this point. If you do, awakening is close at hand.

Buddhist analogy that describes this leaning back is about the difference between a dog and a tiger (I don't hang out with tigers, so I have to take their word for this). Supposedly when you throw meat in front of a dog, it chases the meat. But when you throw meat in front of a tiger, it turns around to see where the meat came from. Leaning forward is like being the dog, and leaning back is like being the tiger. Tigers are more powerful.

You can start this leaning-back process in your regular meditation. Sometimes I like to do this when I'm meditating outside. The spaciousness of the outdoor environment reminds my brain of the spaciousness of awareness. There seems to be a correlation between feeling more physical space and creating mental space, which is also why awareness-based meditations often ask us to open our eyes and gaze straight ahead. To work with leaning back, start by gently lowering the gaze (or closing the eyes) and placing your attention on the breath or the body. When you notice that the mind has left that object, choose to come back to finding your easeful breath. Once you feel a little bit settled (you don't have to feel completely focused to do this, it can just be for a few minutes), you can shift your attention from the breath (the content) to a more open awareness (the context). As you lean back into awareness, you don't focus on any one object of attention. You work with whatever sound, whatever shape, whatever thought might come to visit awareness. You note the experience, but you also note the awareness that's present and holding space for the visitor. If you hear a sound, you don't try to track the sound; you try to track the awareness that is holding space for the sound to arise, dwell, and dissolve. You can play with raising your eyes and gently looking straight ahead during this exercise.

You can do this leaning-back exercise "on the spot," which

is a fancy way of saying "when you're not meditating." You can start with interesting sensory experiences, like eating food. Let's take a raspberry, or any small, tactile, and tasty food. Still your body and eat the berry slowly. As you bite the berry, you can place your attention on the berry itself, and notice the sensory aspects as you eat it (eating a berry may engage at least four senses: sight, touch, smell, and taste). As you note the aspects of the object itself, can you still stay in touch with the "knower," the vivid aspect of awareness that is holding space for this berry experience? How does leaning back and tracking the awareness that knows the berry, rather than tracking the berry itself, change what is experienced?

A trickier on-the-spot practice is leaning back in awareness when you're afraid or angry. Let's take a fear of having a difficult conversation (maybe with a lover, family member, or boss). Let's assume that having this conversation makes you feel anxious but not panicked (if it does, you may need help regulating your nervous system first and foremost). You can take few minutes to sit before the difficult conversation. You might want to practice a loving-kindness meditation for yourself and for the other person. Then bring up the fear or anger. Locate the experience in your body and send attention to that place. If the emotion doesn't feel physical (it usually does, but not always), stay with the mental experience of the feeling. Now, when you can, lean back into awareness. Hold your seat and settle into the awareness that *contains* the fear or anger. Try to stay with this awareness for a few minutes. How does that change the experience? (This exercise might not make the conversation itself any less difficult. That's okay, because some things are just hard.)

Awareness as the Basically Good Parent

The power of awareness involves seeing the mind as a sort of parent for your entire experience. This way of thinking frames the work as a process of slowly learning to parent our internal experience (which is the child), to care for whatever happens internally with unconditional warmth. This approach to meditative awareness follows an observation from the Buddhist psychodynamic thinker Dr. Mark Epstein in which he relates mindful awareness itself to the concept of the "good-enough mother" (an idea first developed by the psychoanalyst D.W. Winnicott in the 1970s). A parent who leans forward too much and obsesses over the child may become a controlling, micromanaging, or even aggressive influence. The child doesn't learn to trust their ability to figure life out from their innate sense of confidence. Likewise, if our mind tries to micromanage all our thoughts and emotions, we can't form a healthy relationship to difficult emotions. On the other hand, if the parent — or awareness — is completely absent, the child doesn't feel held and cared for. Like a parent, when awareness does a basically good, yet imperfect, job of being present, we gain confidence in our ability to work with hard moments. With a basically good relationship to awareness, we can still get lost and caught up in the mind quite a lot. As awareness learns to recognize itself again and again, we learn how to come back. Slowly, the basically good parent of awareness learns to behold whatever arises with warmth and accommodation, intervening only when some action is called for.

I don't know what kind of human parents you had. But with awareness practice, it's possible to slowly learn to re-parent your own mind. The more you come back to awareness, the more your capacity to accommodate every experience — even shame and fear — can grow. And if you learn to accommodate anything you might feel — even those uncomfortable emotions — confidence can develop, even in the hardest of times.

CHAPTER NINE

The Power of Windhorse

We know by now that the winds of the world — pleasure, pain, praise, criticism, fame, insignificance, success, failure — will never stop blowing. Instead of just learning to deal with them, what if we could harness their energy and turn the winds into a power source? What if we could corral the energy of fear and hope and use it all to remind ourselves that we are alive? To do so requires an acceptance of these human experiences and a willingness to make ourselves vulnerable enough to feel them. Developing this capacity involves a set of practices known as *windhorse.*

Windhorse is highly related to the Buddhist concept of *bodhicitta*, or "awakened mind" (also referred to as "awakened heart," because the metaphorical heart and mind are often interchangeable in Buddhist philosophy). Present in both Tantric Buddhism and the Shambhala tradition, it operates on the premise of a power that comes from meeting the forces of life with a tender, brave heart. Windhorse (*ashva-vayu* in Sanskrit, *lung-ta* in Tibetan) incorporates ideas from Confucian thought as well as Indigenous Tibetan shamanism (the pre-Buddhist *bön* tradition). *Wind* represents the forces of life — the eight worldly winds, the forces of karma, and any other energy that moves through us. *Horse* represents our ability to harness and ride those energies. Windhorse is based on the Tantric view that every emotional state is inherently wise, rather than inherently problematic, and on developing confidence within those experiences. It is also based on the idea of taking one's seat and becoming a warrior (or, more literally translated, a heroic or brave person), someone who is open-hearted, willing to face the world head-on with a compassionate presence. This practice isn't about some extreme-sport adrenaline rush. Instead, it's a reminder to use the energy already present in the events of life to become more compassionate and aware.

Joining Heaven and Earth

Windhorse meditation is based on a simple triad with roots in Confucian thought: heaven, earth, and humanity. Earth is the physical world, but more metaphorically, it is the arena of practicality and details. Heaven isn't the afterlife (that's a whole other conversation); it is the arena of creativity and a wider vision of what might be possible. In this framework, the job of humanity is to unify heaven and earth.[1] We humans are called upon to anchor ourselves deeply to the earth while remaining open to the inconceivable vastness of possibility that the cosmos offers. Okay, that's a little grandiose. Grandiosity is what happens when we orient ourselves too much toward heaven and become untethered from the practicalities of earth. Joining heaven and earth is about being creative while also being

1 If you hear Belinda Carlisle lyrics right now, you're forgiven. You're also my kind of person.

practical, visionary while also realistic. Earth is our home, a place we can't ever transcend. At the same time, we aren't shackled to it. We aren't meant to slink our way through life with our heads down.

We see heaven in a great idea for a new art project. We see heaven in an inventor's new solution to a technological problem, in an idea for a company or organization we want to found. We see heaven when a political movement revolutionizes people's ideas of what might be possible for a community or a society. We could think of the act of collective brainstorming as a kind of "heaven" session, getting smart, creative people together and letting them work together to envision new possibilities.

Earth is the realm of washing the dishes in the sink, making your grocery list, remembering to check in on a friend who needs someone to listen, and getting to the dentist (there's nothing more "earth" than that drilling sound). Earth is not the grand vision of your creative project; it's all the details that need to be addressed to make space for that creativity to occur and that vision to come down to Earth. Heaven is where the inspiration occurs, but earth is where most of the work happens. Rather than viewing the details of life as something holding us back from a greater purpose, these warrior teachings view the mundane details as sacred in and of themselves, because they are the stuff of our lives. By connecting with earth when we sit, we transform our relationship with the details of life. We sacralize those parts of adult life that seem like they're just getting in the way of what we wish we were doing.

Honoring the details of life is how we pay our debt to the earth, our original home. Let's face it, the details can be boring, depressing, and sometimes excruciating.[2] Who ever thought, when we were vision-boarding and poeticizing with friends about the life we always wanted to "manifest," that our lives would become mired in so many of these details? Who ever saw all these details in those late-night conversations with our most creative friends about how we were gonna fly right up to the heavens, back to the stardust we all came from, and figure out how to do this thing called existence so differently? Who could ever have seen this slow avalanche of earthiness rumbling toward us as we aged, even if every grown-up we knew told us constantly? We should have seen the beautiful truth of earth in our elders' hair slowly turning a salty gray, in the bags slowly ballooning under their eyes, in the sighs escaping their mouths. And now — in the most predictable surprise imaginable — the same thing is happening to me.

By connecting to the earth as an energetic principle during our windhorse meditation practice, we can start to treat all the mundane aspects of life as sacred. The dentist, the phone call to that friend we haven't made time for, the shuffling through the aisles of a grocery store, the annoying ding of the email inbox when we thought we'd already answered all our emails for the day. When we connect with the earth principle, we shift our relationship to the work we do to hammer out life's details. They become part of the path that leads us to experience life as sacred, instead of being the tedious shackles that hold us back from "manifesting" potential.

By including earth in the practice of generating confidence, we also honor our original home. We honor the place

---

2 The classic movie *Office Space* is all about the resentment inherent in a work life with too much earth and absolutely no heaven. It's TPS reports all the way!

we sometimes forget is sacred. To take our seat on the earth in meditation is to bring ourselves back to the present moment and to experience the environment, sense perceptions, and people who are right here. Coming back to the earth is crucial to any creative process, because there's a part of us that longs to already have completed the entire process, that wants to jump ahead to the finished product of our creative vision. When we jump ahead, we get disembodied and scattered, and innovation gets misaligned with what's happening here and now.

In my twenties I started a nonprofit — the Interdependence Project — with a group of friends. We were committed to secular Buddhism, the arts, and various activism, organizing, and service projects. When people heard the general mission statement, they thought it was a big vision, and maybe just a teensy bit too grandiose for our tiny budget. Most of the work of building that community was in the earthy details: setting up a bank account, finding a lawyer to help us file all the paperwork needed to get our 501(c)(3) status, the seemingly endless emails and meetings that followed — the board meetings, the teacher meetings, the staff meetings, the community meetings, the one-on-one meetings, the editing of programming and curricular documents. Sure, there were visionary moments, but these instances mostly arose in the growing community of all the thoughtful and creative people who gathered to share in what we were doing and gave it life on earth. We had some heavenly ideas for transformative community, but most of the work I did during my stint as executive director involved returning again and again to the details.

Parenthood, I've found, is much the same, albeit less boundaried by the hours of a work schedule and sometimes far more depleting. It's literally one orgasmic moment of heaven to start, with moments of heaven sprinkled in throughout, but mostly it's earthbound details: making sure a growing person is safely navigating the world. You might have a grand notion of bringing new little humans into your household from wherever in the cosmos you believe we came from. You might develop a whole, carefully researched parenting approach as you plan the pregnancy, a strategy that you then post and blog whole manifestos about on social media, sharing your design for physically and mentally healthier humans, your new paradigm for development that will surely be less traumatizing and more enlightened than what the last generation of parents did to us. And then, when it happens, you land back on earth with a thud, to the accompaniment of wails. Parenthood is a toddler who needs a diaper change when there's no bathroom anywhere around (there's no substance more earthy than toddler poop), the sleep deprivation, the appointments, the logistics of coparenting, the making of meals and packing of snacks and packing of backup snacks in case the kids refuse to eat the meals and snacks you initially packed, the delicate negotiations to put their coat back on when it's objectively too cold outside for them to take it off. It's trying to figure out if you and your partner can still be friends while working as the unpaid codirectors of the unincorporated nonprofit organization called This Kid. Parenting is an endless earth dance, and if you don't feel resourced enough to befriend the minutiae, you will suffer mightily.

Either we gradually learn to appreciate the details of life, or we resent them (often it's some mix of both). When we resent the details, it's usually because we have romanticized heaven while feeling trapped on the earth, which is — by definition — a confusing way for an earthling to feel. This imbalance makes us resent the work of showing up every day. It doesn't matter what you're trying to "manifest," dear influencers; it's only in the everyday work that awakening becomes possible.

Let's take the example of doing your taxes. Doing your taxes is an earthy experience. For some people, filing taxes brings up long-held anxiety related to money and feeling resourced. For some, it brings up a sense of inadequacy related to math. For the conservative person in each of us, taxes bring up the grudge of having to pay an oppressive and inefficient entity called the government for services that go to fulfill the needs of people who didn't "earn" it, people who aren't in our family and don't look like us. For progressive people like me, taxes bring up resentment about how much of our shared wealth goes to the military, or how little goes to public education, healthcare, and mental health, or how the ultrawealthy always seem to pay taxes at an obnoxiously lower rate. Regardless of political affiliation, everyone feels stuck in the mud of tax season, and there's rarely any heaven or vision to the process at all.

Noam Chomsky talks (in his own language) about what doing your taxes might look like from the vantage of joining heaven and earth. Chomsky positions taxes — in a healthy democratic society — as an act of collective generosity. He says: "In a [true] democracy, the day when you pay your taxes, April 15, would be a day of celebration, because you're getting together to provide resources for the programs you decided on."[3] I think about this quote when it's time to get my taxes together. Rather than just getting bogged down in the resentment of my

3 Industrial Workers of the World interview with Noam Chomsky, https://archive.iww.org/history/library/Chomsky/2009int/.

limited political and financial agency, I look up and remember the vision of real democracy as an act of shared generosity, and open my heart to that possibility. I contemplate the lovely public park near my house, or my parents' Medicare coverage, or my postal worker, or Tina the crossing guard, my daughter's public school and libraries. I take a second to imagine a world with more social workers than prison guards, more solar panels than guns, fewer bombs dropping on children. These contemplations allow me to raise my gaze and experience something beyond my little corner of numerical anxieties. That's heaven. Then I can address the details with a tiny infusion of aspiration rather than a cloud of claustrophobia.

When you feel mired and weighed down by the practicalities of earth, you come to disdain the absence of heaven. On the other hand, when you feel overly engrossed by the creative vision of heaven, you disembody yourself and forget to relate to all the things that anchor you to life as it is. Some visionaries have a very hard time addressing details. You don't eat as well, you don't care for yourself. Whenever heaven and earth feel out of balance, it's no longer possible to act with much purpose. You lose confidence, because confidence comes from joining the two forces. And that's where windhorse meditation comes in. Windhorse meditation is a very quick practice for joining heaven and earth, and riding whatever emotional "wind" we're experiencing, showing up to whatever comes next with balance and vision.

Rousing Windhorse

Windhorse meditation includes a wide range of practice techniques. The example below is one that I received and taught in the currently inactive Shambhala training program. It's structured to be a brief practice, taking one to five minutes. I often practice it when I need to remember my confidence before speaking to a group, or before a session with a student in distress. If you meditate in the morning, this practice can begin or end a longer meditation session and create a little power-up as you head into the day. You can extend it, especially the second step, depending how much you feel you need to slow down and ground yourself, but it's meant to be brief. In the instruction, we see the three elements of earth, heaven, and humanity, but you don't need to analyze their meaning too much while you sit. We study and analyze when we're reading and contemplating, but when we're meditating, it's much more important to *feel*.

First, take your seat. As you arrange your posture on the cushion or chair, feel yourself claiming your spot on the earth. You get a spot. No more or less than one. You belong here. You can show up. If there are any lingering thoughts about your to-do list or events of the day, see if you can decide, gently but decisively, to set them down for the next few minutes. These thoughts may come back, but intentionally releasing whatever is on your mind is important for coming fully into your seat. When you feel you've claimed your seat, quickly let go of any final lingering thought for this brief meditation.

Second, feel earth, followed by heaven. Take a moment to feel the earth beneath you, supporting you, providing your human embodiment. Feel each part of your body (knees, pelvis, fingertips) as connected and grounded. The earth is what anchors us. You can do this for just a few seconds, or for longer. Next, open your senses to the periphery of the place you're sitting, so you experience that spacious quality of heaven. You can even raise your gaze straight ahead if you like. Notice how it feels to rest in that space.

Third, join heaven and earth at the heart center. See if you can quickly focus attention — gently but fully — on your heart, almost as if a tea-light candle suddenly lit up there. For a short time, focus entirely on the heart center as a physical, energetic center. Your attention to the heart can be concentrated, but not aggressive. Your shoulders can stay relaxed. If your eyebrows furrow, relax them! This step is sometimes called "switching on." It only has to last for ten or fifteen seconds.

Fourth, soften and feel your genuine heart. Soften the concentration, but stay with your awareness of the heart. Feel whatever you feel. Don't overanalyze. If you notice an emotion, or just a flavor of experience, allow that to be there and note it. If you feel tender or vulnerable, be with that. If one of the worldly winds is striking right now, just note that and let it be.

Fifth, radiate confidence from the heart center. At this point, raise your gaze to the horizon and feel the heart as gentle but powerful. Starting from the energetic center of the heart (like a Care Bear, if you need the visual) let your awareness diffuse outward in all directions, including above, below, and behind your body. Don't push from the heart, just let awareness spread like waves in all directions. Rest in awareness for a few moments.

If you want to close by offering yourself a little bow or some other act of acknowledgment that you're showing up to your life as best you can, please do that. A bow can also be a quick way to acknowledge others, acknowledge the earth, and acknowledge the lineages that live within you.

If you want to practice windhorse even more quickly (in two minutes or less), you can very quickly still your body and practice only steps 3–5 in the sequence. Regardless, the themes of heaven, earth, and what it means to join them together in your practice, your work, and your life are helpful to contemplate on a regular basis.

CONCLUSION

The Question of Confidence

One time I attended a lecture on collective liberation by the great teacher Reverend angel Kyodo williams, the coauthor of *Radical Dharma*. She gave a bold and beautiful talk about the true ideal of the bodhisattva, pointing out that if we truly embraced the idea that our awakening is dependent on each other, then we must care about social and racial justice. She gave this talk in front of a predominantly white audience, which is an inherently brave thing for a queer Black woman to do. When it came time for the Q&A, Reverend angel stated plainly, "Ask me anything you want. I'm not fragile." Now, only she can know whether she truly has no fragility in her being. Everyone who has any sort of public persona has learned a trick or two to perform our vulnerability rather than actually making ourselves vulnerable. But Reverend angel conveyed such a relaxed clarity in that moment that it made me think, "Now that, that right there is how I want to be as a teacher and person."

When I write about Buddhism, I try to include myself and my own, occasionally confused, experiences in the offering. I understand, in doing this, that the memoiresque quality of my writing may come across as self-centered to some. But over the years, I have found myself more able to connect with teachers in the psychological, spiritual, or wellness spaces who bring their own struggles into the insights they share. Otherwise, we spiritual writers look like we are hovering above the fray of life, when in fact every bit of genuine insight we might have comes from immersing ourselves fully in the struggle of being human.

Like many, I've studied different methods and traditions for connecting with myself, connecting with others, and connecting with reality. There's never only one source of wisdom. Still, Tantric Buddhism continues to be my primary anchor for trying to live a decent human life. The main reason Tantric Buddhist teachings have always spoken to my heart is that they frame emotional experience as inherently wise and unproblematic. They introduce the view that every state of mind, and every emotion, contains the expression of a form of wisdom. In the absence of self-fixation, that emotion is experienced as healthy, intelligent, and helpful. But when self-regard grows brittle and defensiveness sets in, the coemergent energy manifests as a confused, stuck, and harmful pattern of behavior.

The willingness to be vulnerable is one such coemergent experience. When a defensive ego is vulnerable, it becomes fragile and insecure. We feel exposed, naked on the first day of school, like the universe caught us in a big "gotcha" moment. We want to protect "me and mine" against the rawness of experience. Nobody particularly likes to feel undefended, exposed, or naked. When we're fragile and defensive, that rawness becomes an unbearable sensation. And when something becomes unbearable, our survivalist alarms go up. We defend against vulnerability either by saying "Nothing to see here," and counterattacking the source of the raw feeling, or else we run away and hide, doing whatever we can to stop feeling so compromised. Feeling exposed, we might go in the opposite direction and say, "I'm so sorry! You're right! Look at me! I suck! I suck with the most suckitude that a person has ever sucked!" This kind of overpersonalizing when we're feeling exposed is a self-aggressive way to avoid feeling vulnerable. Self-aggression has a very odd logic: if I beat myself up more than anyone else possibly can, at least I'll be protected from anyone else's attacks. Yet self-aggression is how our self-protection operates much of the time. Whatever the manifestation of defensiveness might be, when we defend against vulnerability, we become less transparent and less available to ourselves and others.

I try to address the issue of my own vulnerability by bringing transparency to myself and my work, as much as I am able to with my own blind spots and defended places. The classic Buddhist teachings list the many traits that identify an enlightened person. The one that has always moved me the most is that an awakened being acts the same whether in private or in public. So if these practices work, they should make us more transparent to ourselves as well as to others.

This way of being open about who you are is a middle path. When I am working with students, I don't want to make them feel like they need to take care of me. That's not my role in their lives. I don't share any of my personal processes publicly until they already feel, well, processed. I have my own dharma mentors, close friends, and a great therapist for that. As the dharma teacher Gina Sharpe once said wisely when the topic of transparency came up at a meditation teacher training, "Transparency is not exhibitionism." Still, I've found repeatedly that sharing my process — to an appropriate degree — humanizes this journey. It helps show how we are each working with our stuck places, meeting our insecurities, and slowly transforming defensiveness into true power. True power is not rigid, it's tender. Because of the power dynamics that have ruled our world for centuries, it feels especially important for people who look like me to practice being vulnerable as much as we can. Supportive groups and *sanghas*, such as racial affinity groups, men's affinity groups, and other communal support structures, are helpful in beginning the process. We've already tried to be confident and strong without making ourselves vulnerable, and look around — that approach didn't work. To find strength in transparency and vulnerability is far more sustainable than trying to erect a house of cards to withstand the worldly winds.

The Question of Power

I recently spoke with a dharma student in Los Angeles whose labor union, the Writers Guild of America, went on strike. The guild includes most of the writers who create our favorite stories for TV, movies, news, and online media. In other words, they create much of the content we love to stream when we're avoiding meditating. At issue in the strike — as is so often the case in our world — were drastically different views regarding power: determining whose work was valued the most in a collaborative, interdependent process of storytelling and media. Also at stake was the protection of the jobs of writers against the incursions of artificial intelligence, which is an existential issue confronting us all in this precarious moment.

Nobody has ever come up with a perfectly designed system for distributing wealth or power that satisfies every last person. Power is hard to distribute because of greed, yes, but also because value and effort are highly subjective and open to interpretation. Conflicting views on who should hold wealth and power in any collaborative process are generally inevitable, even when everyone involved has a compassionate heart and is simultaneously considering the well-being of themselves and others. Clearly, that's not the enlightened world we live in (yet), so in our world these conflicts over resources often turn into manipulative, one-sided struggles for dignity and even for basic survival.

My student is a younger but experienced writer whose career is starting to develop its own power, so the labor strike came at a difficult time for the "seat" she was taking in her industry. She spoke of the risks of going on strike, how if the strike dragged on (as she expected), it might significantly affect not only her own well-being, but the lives of others less established in the field, along with the lives of those in other sectors of her industry. She also spoke of her own shaky confidence in taking up space and proclaiming her needs. "I'm dealing with a lot of shame and internalized capitalism," she said. She wondered if she should just consider herself lucky to make *any* sort of living as a creative, take what was offered, work harder, and be grateful. She was grappling with the twenty-first century winds of success and failure, as well as the question of interdependence, considering the needs of both self and other. As we were chatting, I looked up the compensation packages of some studio executives. Netflix, for example, has two CEOs, and their annual compensation package earns them *each* about $35 million to $50 million a year. That's approximately one hundred times what a highly successful senior TV writer might make, which is in turn, several times more than what a schoolteacher or nurse might make. We could spend a lot of time pondering whether storytelling is genuinely valuable to society. My student and I agreed that it was certainly valuable, and also that teaching school was far more valuable than our society considers it to be. "But let me ask you something," I said. "Do you think the CEO of Netflix is sitting on his meditation cushion right now asking himself 'Am I really worth all this money?'"

The question of confidence isn't just a personal question. It's both political and social, related to who holds seats of power on planet Earth. The themes in this book can't be separated from living in a country where one of the greatest historical examples of the wrong kind of self-confidence, Donald Trump, somehow slid into the White House and for four years was leader of the most powerful country that has ever existed. Another recent example was the sight of megabillionaire Jeff Bezos sitting inside a rocket while his scientists (not him) recreated a feat NASA had achieved sixty years ago: traveling up into the (lower) heavens in the most phallic vessel imaginable, thereby killing irony for good and demonstrating that confident action without compassionate intent will forever lead humanity in the wrong direction.

I sometimes get accused of politicizing Buddhism. My response is that I don't know what the word *politicize* means. Buddhism is certainly about the individual working to root out their own confusion and take responsibility for their mental experience. That personal work is utterly crucial. But in examining reality, we quickly come to see that our individual experience is shaped by our relationships, both our formative relationships and our relationships to society. Our sense of self is dependent on the systems and cultural environment we live in. To be a citizen of democracy — which did not widely exist for the first several millennia of Buddhist practice — is to hold ourselves, and each other, accountable for vocal and active participation in our society. If we pay attention, we see the deep intertwining of our personal experience with the shared realities of our world. You can't politicize a reality that is already political.

At its heart, confidence is a political discussion precisely because it's a discussion of power: who gets to hold it, who doesn't, and why. If mindful people avoid discussing power — if we consider power to be dirty, scary, or just plain greedy — then who inherits the earth? If people who try to be present, ethical, and compassionate do not also manifest self-confidence, we lose the powers of voice, influence, and resources — the agency it takes to make a difference. In our attempt to transcend negativity, we abandon this world to the selfish, the narcissistic, the abusive, and the bloated, those who aren't afraid to take up far more space than is either earned or necessary, those who mistreat others and use the resources of this planet like a toddler breaking his toys the day after his parents bought them. Patriarchy, white supremacy, gross wealth inequality, and environmental catastrophe are problems that arise when the wrong kind of confidence is placed in spiritually immature hands. The outcome has been nothing other than a planetary disaster. In the timeless words of Martin Luther King Jr., "We have guided missiles and misguided men."

Whether or not his broader political movement ultimately fades from power, Trump's presence will persist as a human avatar of the wrong kind of confidence. Trumpism, that "fake-it-until-they-give-it-to-you-while-you-call-them-names" approach to confidence has inherited much of the earth. The tactic of using arrogance to get ahead preceded (and will outlive) him, but invoking his oddly orange visage gets the point across more than any other example of the wrong kind of confidence. If the mindfulness movement doesn't lead to the empowerment of mindful people to organize politically, to negotiate fair contracts, to build compassionate systems, to create artistic movements, to imagine new narratives of personal and collective success, and to claim and share human power more equitably, then all these ancient teachings merely become a way for us to disappear, to abdicate our seats. Instead of showing up, we escape, and we do so at exactly the moment when the world needs us all to confront and dismantle narcissistic motivations for power. Worse, as some theorists like Slavoj Žižek have speculated, meditation practice and Buddhist teachings could become propaganda tools employed by a powerful minority to keep everyone else in a perpetual state of passive transcendence, breathing easefully in a VR meditation hall or yoga studio, while the physical world is ransacked by the insecure and the greedy.

It's scarily easy to imagine meditation becoming a tool for an autocrat to help people cope with no longer having a political voice in their society. As mindfulness skyrockets in popularity, the movement away from the gritty beauty of the real world we all inhabit has lingered in the collective consciousness as a popular — if not dominant — conception of meditation, Buddhism, and spiritual practice in general. Recently, the salute to collective disembodiment seems to have intensified. Meditation apps, led by Calm and Headspace, are now juggernauts, a multibillion-dollar phenomenon. While the spread of these tools is excellent news, we need to be clear about the reasons we practice mindfulness — our view and intention about what we want to do with the practice. In the decade preceding the COVID pandemic, countless magazine covers and Instagram feeds featured images of beautiful people (very often beautiful *blond* people) finding peace from the trials and tribulations of the world through mental escapism. These lean, cross-legged folks" are usually somewhere you are not — an aspirational beach, a lush forest. A well-sculpted mouth is blowing gently on a groomed orchid, a remote and exotic setting is dappled in retouched light with appropriate filters. The meditating model is almost always closing their eyes and going to some galaxy far, far away. One startup meditation center in New York embraced the language of escapism wholeheartedly and unapologetically with its adoption of the name Inscape. A defanged form of mindfulness seems to be the most culturally comfortable and commodifiable. Meanwhile, people who are poorly equipped for leadership continue to run wild on Earth, all because they're willing to grab spotlights and dare the rest of us to do anything about it. Confidence is a spiritual discussion with political teeth, and we shouldn't hide from that sharpness. We should engage with it.

I have no idea what the answer is for my hypothetical question: do the CEOs of Netflix ask themselves difficult questions about their wealth and power? I've never met the CEOs of Netflix. Maybe they suffer from impostor syndrome, but I imagine they probably work hard and are fairly competent at what they do. Maybe they donate a whole bunch to charity. Maybe they even meditate and read Pema Chödrön and Brené Brown to carry them through when life gets hard. So many people do these things now. CEOs certainly don't work hundreds of times harder than anyone else, but within them beat human hearts, just like anyone else, and they get up in the morning and try to navigate their anxiety about mortality, success, and failure as best they can, just like everyone else. Whatever internal process they might go through to be able to assume their opulent seats in this world, seats that are astronomically larger and fancier than those of their employees, they've clearly decided it's okay to hold that amount of power. Maybe they believe that's the best way to help humanity; maybe they've read Joseph Campbell and convinced themselves they're on a hero's journey. I don't have the empathetic imagination to understand how these men would reach such grandiose conclusions if they embarked on a true contemplative process that incorporated compassion and interdependence. Asking questions about your own power is a hard process. Asking these questions of powerful people in public tends to raise a lot of defensiveness. The best way to justify unearned power is to avoid being asked questions about it. And the very best way to avoid a question is to never ask it of yourself.

Warning: contemplation and curiosity make it much harder to avoid asking yourself questions about the relationship between vulnerability, confidence, and power. Spiritual bypassing — using our spiritual practice to avoid hard questions rather than confront them — is something we have to watch out for, of course, but when we hold our seats and make ourselves vulnerable to the winds of the world, we become curious about how power really works, both internally and externally.[1] This contemplative curiosity alone is transformative to the basic dynamic of power. You discover genuine questions: How much do I need? What is it that I really want in order to fulfill my longings? How can I empower others in turn? These are the questions that we need to bring into our shared conversations, because these are the shared contemplations that make power consensual and, in turn, trustworthy. Exactly how much power should each of us try to hold when we take our seats? The answer varies with the context. But with transparency, we ask healthy questions about our power, and in turn, we ask healthy questions about the power structures of this world. We notice our own defensiveness, and we notice the defensiveness of others.

When power becomes uncurious about itself, it takes more confused form — which is to say bloated arrogance, just like a balloon. Balloons take up space, but they're easier to knock around in the wind, and eventually, they pop. In this sort of state, we have less interest in true self-reflection, and certainly no interest in vulnerability. Vulnerability is our ally when we're trying to wake up, but dangerous when we're trying to stay comfortable. This confused approach to power can make our world unbalanced and unsustainable. The kind of compassion we need is more fierce, more daring, more straightforward. Fierce compassion knows how to say no with love and how to leverage the kind of strength it takes to pop the balloon of arrogance. I hope the successful writers' strike leads to other loving demonstrations of power, and that it teaches everyone involved

---

1 The phrase spiritual bypassing was coined by the Buddhist psychotherapist John Welwood. I dive more deeply into that topic in *The Road Home*.

to fearlessly ask for what they need and want, to consider each other, and to consider the world.

Another spiritual danger involves suppressing our worldly longings. We often ignore personal needs out of a misunderstanding of what Buddhism and related spiritual traditions have to say about desire. It's a common misconception that after stepping onto the spiritual path, we're no longer supposed to want to accomplish anything, be anything, or succeed at anything. The problem is that I've never met a person who didn't want to succeed at *something*. That includes every mindfulness practitioner as well as every spiritual teacher I've ever met, myself included. People who claim they have no longings are either lying, numb from previous disappointments, or else they're nihilists, which is a lie that turned itself into a philosophy. Always beware the person who claims to have no desires at all.

This book has been based on the premise that it's okay to want success, happiness, and acknowledgment, especially if we stay present with our feelings and learn to frame the intention for success as an honest yearning to help others as well. When we pretend that what we want to accomplish in life doesn't matter to us, we merely hide our true intent, and the only transcendent experience we end up manifesting is a tremendous amount of passive aggression.

To be fair, this same idealization of disappearance characterizes many classic mythologies of the Tantric Buddhist traditions I practice. In Tibet, advanced yogis could leave their social affairs behind and go deep into meditative retreat in order to pursue something called the Rainbow Body, a state in which the meditator becomes so awake that their body literally disappears into a colorful spectrum of luminosity, leaving only hair and fingernails behind as evidence of the feat. For anyone trying to bolt from the many disappointments and debts of human existence, this image of painless evaporation into a color wheel is alluring.

Occasionally retreating from the world is wise. There's nothing wrong with a mindfulness practice that helps you get space and time away from it all, or with using the support of an app to calm your nerves. So many people receive benefit from practicing meditation. Relieving personal stress is often a more grounded and sincere inspiration for beginning a practice than the aspiration to free all beings from suffering. It's one of my own primary motivations for practice and study. The world is stressful, and learning to access your parasympathetic nervous system to calm yourself is a wonderful thing. Ultimately, however, sticking with such a limited approach becomes just that, a limitation. Retreats are a valuable part of anyone's spiritual journey, but they should be thought of as preparation for life, not disappearance from it.

Doing Hard Things

We all do hard things every day. Some of them are small enough — and the demands of life large enough — that we do them without much acknowledgment or complaint, without patting ourselves on the back. For me, parenting feels that way. Whatever is required of me as a father, I show up for that, and I trust in my basic goodness to see and fulfill my child's needs. "Dad life" feels intuitive for me. Other things are much harder to do. What's hard for you is a personal question, and we each need validation of our efforts to show up. For many people I know, regular meditation is one of those small hard things to do regularly. If you struggle to sit with your mind and body, if you feel like your meditation seat is wobbly and your practice is light-years from perfect, you probably deserve more credit than you give yourself for taking on the struggle to hold that seat. Meditation can be simple, but it is rarely easy. It's an example of the millions of ways it's hard to show up in daily life.

Other hard things are big, looming, scary, and downright overwhelming to your heart and your nervous system. While I was writing this book, I decided to take on one of my own big hard things, a thing which — odds are — isn't a very big deal to you at all: I got my driver's license.

When I was young, I was overwhelmed by the prospect of driving. I also froze up while taking certain types of tests. My anxieties, along with insufficient practice on the stressful streets of the largest city in America, led me to fail my road test. And then I went to college, where freshmen weren't allowed to have cars, and I couldn't afford one anyway. Why get my license? I thought, resisting the fear of taking my seat again behind the wheel. And then I was in my twenties. And somehow my twenties became my thirties, which became my early forties, and even though I traveled constantly, I always relied on friends, partners, airplanes, and mass transit to move me from A to B. Even with all the other hard things I was showing up for in life, I never took my seat behind the wheel.

The fact that I could always get by without doing this particular hard thing was a convenient excuse, but it undoubtedly made my life much less convenient, which is how convenient excuses generally operate. As I got further and further into adulthood, my shame at not having embraced this challenge thickened into a sort of mental plaque. Finally, for a variety of reasons (one being the desire to practice what I was preaching while writing a book with the ambitious title *Confidence*), I decided to take on this challenge, and transform my experience of decades of perceived failure to take my seat.

With intention, I tried to employ the four principles I've described in this book. I brought awareness to the shame and fear I was feeling and made sure to disclose them to myself and others in order to normalize and work with that fear and vulnerability. I called on my invisible lineage of heroic beings and ancestors, asking for their support, including my Grandma Claire, who had also gotten her driver's license later in life. I practiced compassion meditation for the younger me who had frozen up, overwhelmed by this challenge. I tried to lean back into my awareness without running away from the moment at hand. When I started to practice driving, I first did it with a good and supportive friend to whom I could tell my history. "Thanks for telling me what's up," he said. "I won't judge you. You're gonna be fine." I quickly raised windhorse and let the car roll out of its parking spot and into the daunting streets of Brooklyn. I drove for almost forty-five minutes that first time out, and watched the amorphous beast of my fear turn into a group of manageable experiences I could break down into bite-sized pieces. Over five weeks, I practiced almost every day. I discovered I really liked driving!

When the day of my road test came, I returned to practicing loving-kindness meditation for my seventeen-year-old self. I started out by making a silly mistake. After checking my mirrors and blind spot perfectly, somehow I neglected to shift from Park to Drive as I tried to pull away from the curb. "Wrong gear!" the by-the-book DMV inspector barked at me. I knew from my few driving-school lessons — where they meticulously explained the point system of the road test and told us that the average person has to take the test three to five times in New York City before passing — that even this nondangerous mistake would cost me points right off the bat. This fact would have flooded the brain of seventeen-year-old me, and it would have been game over for that kid. But forty-four-year-old me had better tools. I breathed, acknowledged my nerves aloud, and shifted gears smoothly. Then I drove flawlessly the rest of the way. I passed the test with points to spare. And I drive now. A lot. Driving is fun and liberating. I can hold the driver's seat. That big scary thing has become just a thing I do.

Practicing the principles of mindfulness, awareness, compassion, and windhorse in no way guarantees immediate success out there in the world. So when I signed up for the driver's test, I had already resolved that if I failed, I'd just sign up to take it again a few weeks later. If my life over the last few years has had one core spiritual message, it's been that life almost never — repeat, never — goes according to plan. In this case, however, I was able to achieve the result I wanted, and it only took me an extra twenty-seven years (a very short amount of time in Buddhist terms!).

Regardless of outcome, these practices of confidence can influence our internal experience, and they remind us to show up and hold our seats when the winds of life start knocking us around. The more we hold our seats — especially if we hold them with concern for both self and others — the more basically good things tend to happen to us. And even if we "fail" at a given endeavor, these practices transform our experience of what it means to succeed or fail. We tend to grasp a little less at the outcome of any one event and focus on the larger picture, a picture that is galactically bigger than the myopic view of any one achievement or loss.

The eight worldly winds are whispering and shouting at you all the time. When you're able to welcome them as frequent guests, you can feel your way toward holding your seat without needing to defend against your own experience. When I take my seat, questions about the best way to show up in a given situation (what Buddhists sometimes call "skillful means") become more immediate, more embodied, and less theoretical. In each exchange, I ask, *What is it appropriate to do for my own well-being? What is my location within this relationship or group? How can I be aware of the power dynamics involved? What is the best way to help empower others in this process?* The answers to these questions are quite different depending on whether I'm taking my seat as a teacher, a mentor, a friend, a parent, a romantic partner, a creative person, or a citizen of a democracy. Sometimes my chosen approach ends up revealing my blind spots just as much as it reveals any skill on my part, but I try to keep asking the questions nonetheless. Your tender humanity will be present in all of the many seats you hold in your life, and you'll be touched by the winds of the world no matter how you might try to shield your heart against them.

By making ourselves curious about the unknown, we touch the most important aspect of being human, which is a longing to become more connected to ourselves and others. And when we touch in with this curiosity regularly, we can commit to empowering other people on their journeys as well. With curiosity, confidence becomes less of an elusive recipe of boldness and toxic bravado and more of a gentle practice of settling into the gusty winds of experience that we can embrace on any given day of our lives.

You are here. This is happening. Take your seat.

Acknowledgments

First and foremost, I've always wanted to thank the reader. Giving something your attention is such a rare gift. So thank you for reading this book, and for taking the time you took with it. It's deeply appreciated.

Thanks to my parents, Janice Ragland and David Nichtern, who introduced me to the path. Thanks to my teachers for their wisdom over the years. There are too many to name, but I'd especially like to thank Dzogchen Ponlop, Sharon Salzberg, Gaylon Ferguson, David Dumais, and Suzann Duquette.

Thanks to my agents, Ellen Scordato and Lisa Weinert, for all their amazing work, and for convincing me that I wasn't quite sick of writing just yet, and just maybe won't ever be. Thanks to my editor, Jason Gardner, along with my publicist, Kim Corbin, and everyone else at New World Library for all your insights and efforts. Thanks to Lisa Braun Dubbels for your counsel on this work as well.

Thanks to all the many friends who have been so supportive during the productive chaos of recent years, especially Jerry Kolber, Lou Sharma, Maho Kawachi, Heather Coleman, Josh Ritter, Adjowah Scott, Shelly Tygielski, Seth Freedman, Jamie Isaia, David Perrin, Shanté Paradigm Smalls, Chris Child, and Kassi Underwood.

Thanks to Marissa Dutton for being such a dear friend and an unbelievable mom and coparent.

And finally, thanks to all the many dharma students I work with who show me their own confidence each time we share space. More than anything else, it was from listening to your individual insights — and your collective wisdom — that this book came into being.

About the Author

ETHAN NICHTERN IS THE AUTHOR of four other books, including *The Road Home: A Contemporary Exploration of the Buddhist Path* and *The Dharma of "The Princess Bride": What the Coolest Fairy Tale of Our Time Can Teach Us about Buddhism and Relationships*. He is also the host of the popular podcast *The Road Home*.

Since 2002, Ethan has taught meditation and Buddhist psychology classes and workshops around North America and Europe. He founded the Interdependence Project and was a shastri, or senior teacher, in Shambhala International from 2010 to 2018. He currently works with students privately and conducts a full schedule of Buddhist studies classes online via the DharmaMoon.com platform.

He is based in Brooklyn, New York, where he lives with his daughter.

More info on Ethan is available at EthanNichtern.com and DharmaMoon.com